Virtue Ethics

BLOOMSBURY ETHICS SERIES

Bloomsbury Ethics is a series of books written to help students explore, engage with and master key topics in contemporary ethics and moral philosophy.

Series Editors: Thom Brooks, Department of Politics, University of Newcastle, UK and Simon Kirchin, Department of Philosophy, University of Kent, UK.

Available now:

Intuitionism, David Kaspar
Reasons, Eric Wiland

Forthcoming in the series:

Autonomy, Andrew Sneddon
Moral Motivation, Leonard Kahn
Moral Realism, Kevin DeLapp
Trust, Ethics and Human Reason, Olli Lagerspetz

BLOOMSBURY ETHICS

Virtue Ethics

NAFSIKA ATHANASSOULIS

BLOOMSBURY
LONDON • NEW DELHI • NEW YORK • SYDNEY

Bloomsbury Academic

An imprint of Bloomsbury Publishing Plc

50 Bedford Square	175 Fifth Avenue
London	New York
WC1B 3DP	NY 10010
UK	USA

www.bloomsbury.com

First published 2013

British Library Cataloguing-in-Publication Data
A catalogue record for this book is available from the British Library.

ISBN: HB: 978-1-4411-1819-6
PB: 978-1-4411-2672-6

Library of Congress Cataloging-in-Publication Data
Athanassoulis, Nafsika, 1973-
Virtue ethics / Nafsika Athanassoulis.
p. cm. – (Bloomsbury ethics)
Includes bibliographical references (p.) and index.
ISBN 978-1-4411-1819-6 (hardcover: alk. paper) – ISBN 978-1-4411-2672-6
(pbk.: alk. paper) – ISBN 978-1-4411-4004-3 (ebook pdf: alk. paper) –
ISBN 978-1-4411-6287-8 (ebook epub: alk. paper) 1. Ethics. 2. Virtue. I. Title.
BJ1521.A68 2012
171'.3–dc23
2012015688

Typeset by Deanta Global Publishing Services, Chennai, India
Printed and bound in India

For NKT and LCK

CONTENTS

Acknowledgements x
Abbreviations, sources and translations xi

Introduction 1

PART ONE Virtue ethics as a new alternative 9

1 Virtue ethics, a revived alternative 11
1. A small revolution 11
2. What do we want from ethics? 14
3. How should I live my life? 16
4. One size does not fit all 18
Further readings 20

2 Ethics and morality 22
1. The limits of morality 22
2. The meaningful life 27
3. Why you don't want to be a moral saint 30
4. How to avoid moral schizophrenia 32
Further readings 34

3 Character and the emotions 35
1. The purity of morality 35
2. The notion of 'character' 39
3. Character development 41
4. The fragility of goodness 44
Further readings 47

Conclusion for Part One 48

PART TWO Virtue ethics comes of age 51

4 Virtue; an Aristotelian definition I 53
    1. The primacy of virtue 53
    2. Doing the right thing is not enough 56
    3. The function of human beings 58
    4. The definition of virtue 61
    Further readings 66

5 Virtue; an Aristotelian definition II 67
    1. The role of the ideally virtuous agent 67
    2. The *orthos logos* 70
    3. Moral perception 71
    4. Practical wisdom 76
    Further readings 80

6 A naturalistic account of virtue 81
    1. Teleology; a discredited account? 81
    2. Aristotle on teleology 85
    3. Moral luck 88
    4. Hursthouse and Foot on teleology 93
    Further readings 96

Conclusion for Part Two 98

PART THREE Current developments in
               virtue ethics 101

7 The challenge from personality psychology 103
    1. The fundamental attribution error 103
    2. Reconsidering the empirical evidence 108
    3. Weakness of will 111
    4. Getting it wrong 117
    Further readings 120

8   Moral education and the virtues 121
1. Failing to notice 121
2. Moral imagination 125
3. The emotions revisited 129
4. Change 133
Further readings 136

9   The Kantian response 137
1. The role of the categorical imperative 137
2. Imperfect duties and impartiality 141
3. Acting from duty and the emotions 143
4. Virtue as strength of will 147
Further readings 151

Conclusion for Part Three 152

Conclusion 157

Notes 160
Bibliography 167
Index 173

ACKNOWLEDGEMENTS

No teaching project is ever possible without the good will and support of the students involved in it. The greatest debt incurred in the writing of this book is owed to all my students whose feedback and patience has been indispensable in developing my teaching ideas. Their feedback because it is impossible to develop one's own philosophical ideas in isolation from others; and their patience as any increase in my abilities has been attained at the inevitable cost of boring a fair number of my captive audience. I would also be remiss not to mention a further debt owed to all my teachers and all my colleagues over the years who have shared their teaching ideas and allowed me to benefit from their good examples.

I am very grateful to Thom Brooks, Kathy de Gama, Simon Kirchin and an anonymous referee for very helpful comments on earlier drafts of this work. I am also particularly grateful to Julia Annas for letting me read a copy of her *Intelligent Virtue* prior to its publication.

Finally, none of this would have been possible without the support of my partner, Christos, and the tacit compliance of my daughter, Lily, who occasionally refrained from crying so I could get some work done.

ABBREVIATIONS, SOURCES AND TRANSLATIONS

Works by Aristotle cited by abbreviation:

DA   *De Anima*, trans. Lawson-Tancred H., (London: Penguin Books, 1986)

DPA   *De Partibus Animalium*, trans. Balme D.N., (Oxford: Oxford University Press, 1992)

NE   *Nicomachean Ethics*, trans. Thompson J.A.K. (London: Penguin Books, 1976)

R   *Art of Rhetoric*, trans. Freese J.H., (Cambridge, Massachusetts: Harvard University Press, 1994)

Citations to Aristotle's works standardly refer to Behher I. (ed.), *Aristotelis Opera* (Berlin, 1831). So that NE 1147a 35, refers to the sentence in the *Nicomachean Ethics* on line 35 of column (a) in page 1147.

Works by Kant cited by abbreviation:

A   *Anthropologie in pragmatischer Hinsicht*
Anthropology From a Pragmatic Point of View (1798), in trans. Gregor M.J., *Anthropology From a Pragmatic Point of View* (Netherlands: Martinus Nijhoff, 1974)

G   *Grundlegung zur Metaphysik der Sitten*
The Groundwork of the Metaphysics of Morals (1785), in trans. Paton H.J., *The Moral Law* (Great Britain: Routledge, 1991)

KpV   *Krtitik der praktischen Vernunft*
       Critique of Practical Reason (1788), in trans. Gregor J.,
       Practical Philosophy (USA: Cambridge University Press,
       1996)

KrV   *Kritik der reinen Vernunft*
       Critique of Pure Reason (1781), in trans. Guyer P. and
       Wood A.W., *Critique of Pure Reason* (USA: Cambridge
       University Press, 1998)

MS   *Die Metaphysik der Sitten*
       The Metaphysics of Morals (1797), in trans. Gregor M.J.,
       The Metaphysics of Morals (Great Britain: Cambridge
       University Press, 1996)

Rel   *Die Religion innerhalb der Grenzen der blossen Vernunft*
       Religion Within the Boundaries of Mere Reason (1793),
       in trans. Wood A.W. and di Giovanni G. (eds), *Religion
       and Rational Theology* (USA: Cambridge University Press,
       1996)

Citations to Kant's works standardly refer to *Kants gesammelte
Schriften, herausgegeben von der Deutschen, Akademie der
Wissenscheften*, 29 vols (Berlin: Walter de Gruyter, 1902).

Introduction

The last couple of decades have seen a shift in perceptions regarding the relationship between research and teaching. There has been a strong emphasis on viewing the two activities as separate, led primarily by managerial concerns aimed at increasing academic efficiency. Excellence in research and excellence in teaching are evaluated separately, funding policies attempt to differentiate between the two and now some academic institutions are beginning to characterize their staff as engaged exclusively in one or the other of these two activities. In philosophy, this distinction between research and teaching is artificial and gravely damaging for the discipline (I imagine a similar case could possibly be made for other disciplines as well).

A simple, but persuasive, definition of philosophy is that it concerns itself with good reasoning. The discipline covers a huge number of topics and has links to all sorts of other subjects, from mathematics to English literature, from music to physics, but what unites all these intellectual activities under the banner of 'philosophy' is that they are all concerned with uncovering good arguments. Because of this, philosophical research and philosophical teaching are identical in their approach. Philosophy researchers are concerned with critically assessing the work of their peers, examining available arguments for weaknesses and omissions and making useful and original contributions to the community's search for truth. They achieve all this by engaging with the work of others, trying out their own arguments by publishing and sharing work with other researchers and, in general, developing their reasoning skills. Philosophical research is a community enterprise, one which depends on the contribution of others and thrives on debate and the exchange of ideas.

Philosophy students are engaged in the same enterprise. Students are taught philosophy by being exposed to it. We learn to think well by thinking and practising our reasoning skills. We expose students to both strong and weak philosophical arguments in the hope that they pick up something about how to construct a critical, original argument. There is a reason that there is no unified philosophy curriculum taught across the world (or even within certain countries) and that is because there is no need for one. What unifies philosophers is not our preoccupation with philosopher P or idea X, but rather our interest in reasoning and good reasoning can be displayed by all sorts of thinkers, on all sorts of topics (and of course we learn as much from criticizing poor reasoning as we do from analysing good reasoning). There is no need for specifying a precise content for the philosophy curriculum because the actual content is not crucial – the development of the reasoning skills is.

In this sense then, the researcher in philosophy and the student of philosophy are engaged in exactly the same enterprise and benefit greatly from viewing their efforts as part of a unified whole. If we artificially attempt to disengage research from teaching, we create divisions where there are none and risk harming both activities. A good teacher will have a good command of the materials she wishes to teach, and this involves understanding how different ideas relate to each other, how opposing views take advantage of each others' weaknesses, which questions remain unanswered, etc. Understanding all this is crucial to relating new ideas to students, and doing so in a way that is comprehensible and clear. At the same time, these are the building blocks of good research. By seeing how different ideas relate to each other, our teacher may be inspired to come up with a new alternative, by focusing on the weaknesses of competing views, our teacher may come up with some new replies to familiar objections, by seeing which questions remain unanswered, our teacher may come up with answers. Our teacher then is indistinguishable from a researcher.

At the same time our student also has to engage with the ideas he is presented with. Simple regurgitation of ideas is catastrophic for philosophical education. If philosophy were simply a matter of learning some facts it could be taught via multiple choice questionnaires, but the small group tutorial – and ideally the one-to-one interaction – remains the ideal method of teaching philosophy because it allows students to really engage with the ideas they come across. Philosophy teachers encourage their students to use the first tense and counsel them to use phrases such as 'I will argue that', 'I will object to', 'I will support claim X', etc. Such phrases illustrate the students' own contribution to the topic, they show that they have not merely encountered the ideas of the course but engaged with them, that is, understood them, criticized them, rejected or approved of them, replaced them or improved on them. Our student is indistinguishable from a researcher in this respect as teaching him philosophy essentially involves developing his philosophical reasoning skills, his research capabilities.

The aim of this volume is to provide a critical introduction to virtue ethics for readers who have some general background knowledge of moral philosophy. An equally important aim of this volume is to reject the research/teaching division and both present materials in a critical manner and expect readers to view them in this manner. This volume is not simply everything one could ever possibly want to know about its subject matter, virtue ethics, but rather represents my own research interests in this area. Ideas are presented through the prism of the author's viewpoint, but they are also presented in a manner which will, hopefully, encourage the readers to develop their own viewpoint. Of course, one practical difference between research and teaching is the level of specialization in one's audience. Students will, on the whole, tend to require materials to be presented at a more introductory level, but this does not preclude a critical approach. A talk aimed at a research audience already intimately familiar with one's topic should be pitched at a different level, for example, assuming background knowledge, but essentially the tasks of the researcher and the teacher are the same: how to critically engage with the ideas and make some, perhaps very modest, contribution to the topic.

In this sense, although the present volume is, in terms of the level it is pitched at, primarily a textbook intended to introduce the student to the main claims of virtue ethics, it also includes elements of a research text, in that it adopts a critical, selective and reflective approach and, hopefully, encourages its readers to do the same. The volume assumes that the reader has an introductory familiarity with normative theories such as deontology and consequentialism (interested readers who lack this degree of familiarity may wish to read up on encyclopaedia articles on normative ethics prior to reading this volume) and proceeds from there to introduce virtue ethics as an alternative to these theories. In what follows, I offer a brief outline of the main ideas discussed in this book.

Outline

Virtue ethics is an umbrella term, covering a variety of different theories and claims, which have their roots in the works of many different philosophers, from Plato and Aristotle to Hume, to Nietzsche and beyond. It would be impossible to give an exhaustive account of all these diverse theories; readers interested in such an approach might wish to consider a number of survey articles and encyclopaedia entries available on all these topics. By contrast, this volume aspires to offer a critical, challenging and reasoned approach to, by necessity, only *some* aspects of virtue ethics. What is lost in scope by this approach should be gained in depth of argument and in encouraging the readers to engage with the ideas which are discussed in a more reflective manner. The kinds of claims which will be examined here fall broadly under the categorization of Aristotelian virtue ethics, probably the most dominant and influential account of virtue ethics in the research literature at the moment. This reflects both the importance of the position itself and my personal research interests.

The volume is divided into three parts, each one of which has a slightly different focus. The first one assumes that the readers have no prior acquaintance with virtue ethics and is structured around the work of the philosophers who first led the revival of interest in virtue ethics in modern moral philosophy. This period of thinking is characterized by a sense of dissatisfaction with the then available alternative normative theories, that is, deontology and consequentialism, and an awareness that something crucial was missing from the debate. Articulating this sense of what was missing, of a different approach which one should take when considering moral matters, of a change in direction in the debates dominating moral theory, gave rise to the main claims of virtue ethics. Part I follows fairly closely the development of these ideas, by considering the works of major philosophers of the period and introducing the reader to their main arguments.

Part I considers the move from asking 'What is the right thing to do?' to asking 'How should I live my life?' and how answering this question also requires a shift from 'rules' and 'obligations' to 'virtues' and 'character'. Unlike rigid, inflexible rules, appeal to virtues can capture the contextual sensitivity of moral situations and the diversity of the moral life. Instead of focusing on what we should do in particular, often bizarre and implausible, moral problems, we should concentrate on developing the right moral character that can respond to all sorts of unpredictable moral situations. This part develops an account of the meaningful life for human beings as a life rich in personal relationships that welcomes the importance of friendships and makes room for partial considerations within the moral sphere, something that deontological and consequentialist theories miss out on.

Finally, this part also considers the concept of 'character' which plays such a central role in virtue ethics and its place in gradual, long term and situationally sensitive moral development. We shall see how the virtue ethical conception of the moral life for beings such as our species is a vulnerable and fragile good, achievable only after years of gradual development subject to external factors and the vagaries of luck.

Readers who are already intimately familiar with virtue ethics may wish to skip directly to Part II, although many of the themes elaborated on and defended in this second part have their roots in the discussions developed in Part I.

The second part of the volume presents and defends a particular account of virtue ethics, one which finds its inspiration in Aristotelian ideas and the concept of the *eudaimon* life. This account also relies on a particular understanding of the virtuous agent as a rare ideal. In this sense, this part is rather selective in that it does not offer a comprehensive account of other alternative accounts of virtue ethics; rather, it seeks to defend one particular version of the theory. There are several themes that will be articulated within this broader tradition of Aristotelian, *eudaimonistic* ethics, but the focus is not on an exhaustive description of all the discussions currently in the literature, rather on a more critical defence of a particular position.

The defence of this account of virtue ethics starts off with the recognition of the central role of 'virtue' and 'character' in the theory. Virtue is central in virtue ethics in two ways: first, moral judgements are judgements of the agent's character and second, the account of the virtues is linked to human nature. We will consider how true virtue requires both the right reason and the right desire and must be chosen, chosen knowingly and chosen for its own sake;

it is therefore an expression of the agent's character and not an accident, a mistake or an action motivated by the wrong reason. Furthermore, we'll see how this account of virtue is based on Aristotle's function argument which asks what is the function of human beings *qua* human beings and finds that reason is the answer, so that virtue is the life of excellence in accordance with reason. This conception of virtue also relies heavily on the understanding of the Doctrine of the Mean as a doctrine of appropriateness, that is, that the appropriate amount of feeling relevant to each virtue is neither too much nor too little, and the right amount is relative to the situation and the individual – it is the role of the virtuous agent to determine what the right amount actually is.

The discussion then moves on to examining the precise role of the virtuous agent. There are a number of problems associated with seeing the virtuous agent as an *actual* role model and guide to virtue, but as we shall see, the virtuous agent is an example of *how* to think and not an actual example of *what* to think. The main characteristic of the virtuous agent is to determine virtue in accordance with the *orthos logos* (right reason). He achieves this through moral perception, the ability to see the morally salient features of each situation, and practical wisdom, the ability to weigh up the different moral demands of each situation. It is these abilities, moral perception and practical wisdom, that we should focus on and it is in this respect that the virtuous agent is an example of *how* to think.

Finally, this part of the book returns to the teleological reasoning behind the function argument examined earlier and asks whether there is any place for teleology in modern debates. It reconsiders Aristotelian teleology and gives a more plausible account of the roots of Aristotle's argument, one which evades many of the critiques that have led modern authors to, on the whole, reject teleology. As part of this renewed interest in teleology, this part concludes with a critical reflection on two recent accounts of teleological ethics, those of Rosalind Hursthouse and Philippa Foot.

The third part of this volume considers current developments in virtue ethics which give us some hints as to the direction of future research in this area. In particular, it examines three themes: the challenge to virtue ethics from personality psychology, some practical considerations regarding moral education in the virtues and the development of modern Kantian theories in response to the concerns raised by virtue ethics.

Chapter 7 considers an objection raised in recent years against virtue ethics which uses evidence from experiments in personality psychology to claim that there are no such things as character traits or, in a different version of the objection, that it is *situational* rather than *dispositional* factors that affect behaviour (not who we are, but what situations we come across). This chapter will respond to the objection in three ways: first, it will suggest that the very evidence itself can be interpreted in different ways within the discipline of personality psychology; aggregation rather than individual instances of behaviour confirm the existence of character traits over time.

Second, I will show how a more nuanced conception of the development of virtue, one that includes the character traits of continence and incontinence, can account for the evidence of the experiments. For Aristotle, it is only the character traits of virtue and vice that are stable, reliable, long-term dispositions, because they both involve choice (one for the good and one for evil) and long-term habituation of one's desires to confirm one's reason. By contrast, continent and incontinent agents exist in a state of struggle between their right reason and their wayward desires. Continence and incontinence are developmental stages, and as such agents fluctuate between them, which is why we do not observe behavioural consistency. Otherwise, continent agents may lapse into incontinence when faced with great challenges, that is, exactly the conditions created by the experiments.

Third, I will argue that rather than being a challenge to virtue ethics, the results of the experiments are a rich source of evidence confirming the main claims of the theory. Aristotelian theory suggests that there are many ways in which one can go wrong and miss the mark of virtue, and this claim is supported by the evidence of the experiments. To conclude the chapter, I will discuss brief accounts of how one can go wrong on the way to virtue, suggesting promising avenues for future research between philosophy and psychology.

Chapter 8 will develop some thoughts on moral education, because education is one of the most important factors in shaping character. Following on from the themes developed in Part II, we will consider what is involved in learning *how* to think, in developing the moral perception and practical wisdom necessary for virtue. The discussion starts by highlighting the importance of noticing moral situations in the first place. Although this may seem self-evident, it is actually the case that many students of morality fail to notice what has moral significance in the real world. This chapter will also highlight the importance of moral imagination and will identify a number of practical ways of sensitizing students to moral requirements and getting them to re-conceive of themselves as part of a morally active world. A section of this chapter deals with the varied and important roles of the emotions in this account of morality, and therefore with what education can do to promote the right emotions. Finally, the chapter concludes with a look at the possibility of change, of how we learn, adapt and develop all through our lives.

The last chapter, Chapter 9, will come full circle and examine the Kantian response to the virtue ethical objections raised in Part I. There are a plethora of diverse answers here but they mainly focus on reinterpreting parts of Kantian theory that can take account of our empirical natures. We will see how, in response to the objection that deontologists rely on rigid rules, neo-Kantians provide more detailed accounts of the Categorical Imperative as a test of subjective maxims, and focus on the importance of imperfect duties which both require judgement for their exercise and allow room for partial considerations such as friendships. We will reconsider the place of emotions in Kantian theory and see how recognition of the moral law has some affective elements, while at the same time modern reinterpretations of Kant allow for a subsidiary role for other emotions as well. Finally, we will examine the Kantian account of virtue and conclude, first, that any comparisons between Aristotle and Kant on virtue have to be sensitive to the richness of their respective theories and second, that one of the fundamental tasks for neo-Kantians is to reconcile Kant's conception of virtue in the intelligible world with his conception of virtue in the sensible world.

PART ONE

Virtue ethics as a new alternative

CHAPTER ONE

Virtue ethics, a revived alternative

1. A small revolution

In 1958, the philosopher Elizabeth Anscombe published a paper that was to change the shape of modern moral philosophy. Until that time, the main debate in moral theory concerning normative theories was between proponents of, broadly conceived, deontological theories and proponents of, broadly conceived, consequentialist theories. As a very general definition, normative theories try to provide some account of what is morally good and right. One of the ways of classifying different normative theories is to divide them between those that give an account of what is right in terms of producing good consequences (broadly speaking, consequentialist theories) and are therefore outcome-based, and those that give an account of what is right in terms of the agent's motives and intentions and are therefore agent-based (broadly speaking, deontological theories). So if you think about an act as a whole (including motives, choices, acting/omitting, results, etc.), consequentialists will focus on an assessment of the results, the consequences of what was done, whereas deontologists will focus on an assessment on what was intended, for example, whether the agent acted from duty. This means that consequentialists and deontologists may come up with entirely different accounts of what we ought to do and whether we should hold people responsible or not for what they have done. For example, if I set out to help a friend by introducing her to someone she likes but unintentionally embarrass her, a deontologist may conclude that what I did was right as I acted out of friendship, but a consequentialist may conclude that what I did was wrong as the result was unpleasant for my friend. This type of debate, whether rightness resides in consequences or intentions, had dominated the main discussions in ethical theory until that time (and had done so, of course, in a manner much more complicated and sophisticated than that suggested by this very simplified example), but Anscombe's paper was to change all this.

Instead of highlighting the differences between consequentialism and deontology, Anscombe focused on a feature that she claimed these two types of theories shared, namely their reliance on rules. She argued that recourse to rules was the wrong conception of ethics. In effect, she advised for a small revolution in the way we think about moral philosophy.

What deontology, consequentialism and most of modern moral philosophy share, according to Anscombe, is a 'law conception of ethics'. That is, a legal understanding of morality, such that 'ought', in a moral sense, is equivalent to 'is obliged to', in a legal sense. The content of the law and the specific obligations it creates may differ, so that, Utilitarians for example will rely on the Greatest Happiness principle, whereas Kantians will focus on the Categorical Imperative, but the structure of the moral theories will be the same. They will all assume this idea of morality as a *legalistic* commandment which is captured in the notions of obligation and duty. So while Utilitarians for example would advise us to perform the action that brings about the best consequences for the greatest number and Kantians would tell us to act only in accordance with maxims that we can will should become universal laws, which are clearly two different ways of acting, the *type* of advice is the same; they are both about what we are obliged to do in the sense of a law or binding regulation.

The main problem with law conceptions of ethics is that they make little sense in the absence of a legislator (Anscombe rejects the Kantian appeal to 'self-legislation' and interprets deontological theories as suffering from the same weaknesses as other conceptions of law ethics). Without a legislator imposing his will, the sense of obligation that is expressed in the moral 'ought' comes under question. This is a very serious objection. The very notion of 'normativity' that normative theories are supposed to account for and explain, involves the idea of a moral ought, of being, in some way, bound to behave in a particular manner. To see this, consider the following distinctions. 'Can I open the window?' is a question about one's abilities, that is, 'Am I strong enough to open the window? Am I tall enough to open the window?' etc., while 'May I open the window?' is a question about permission, that is, 'Am I allowed to open the window?' which assumes that there is someone who will permit or forbid this act. Pedantic English language teachers the world over delight in such distinctions and many a long-suffering student has had to put up with a hot stuffy room because he asked a question about his *ability* to open the window rather than obtaining *permission* to do so! In the same way, 'Ought I (or should I) open the window?' is an entirely different type of question. You may wonder here why opening the window is a moral matter in the first place, but a plausible scenario can be construed within which the 'ought/should' question makes sense. Assume you are walking past a primary school when you notice the building is on fire, the exits are blocked, but there is a ground floor, large window which you could open (the ability question is answered here), without any risk or cost to yourself and which would provide an immediate means of escape for a class of children. In this case 'Ought I open the window?' makes a lot of sense – in fact, most people would immediately and without thought answer 'yes, I should do so' and feel bound to do something about the situation (should you come across people who are tempted to answer 'no' to this kind of question, beware you may be in the presence of a psychopath!).

Moral questions then are questions about normativity, about the force of morality, about why we feel bound to act in a moral manner, but according to Anscombe, by seeing morality as a set of laws which are not backed up by the authority of a legislator, we cannot make sense of the idea of morality binding us to do anything; therefore, neither consequentialism nor deontology can really account for morality's force. Consequentialists and deontologists can frame their advice in the shape of laws, but since morality is not governed by a legislator, they can neither convince us to follow this advice, nor can they account for why we generally find moral demands to be binding.

Instead of relying on this legalistic conception of ethics, Anscombe encourages us to reconsider the way we do ethics, to set aside law

conceptions of ethical theories as implausible and revive elements
of Aristotelian theory. Specifically, she calls for a more central role
for the concept of 'virtue', for reviving the importance of flourishing
in understanding the role of morality in human lives and posits
a radical claim to suspend all discussions of moral philosophy
until we can achieve a better insight into moral psychology. These
suggestions ask for a veritable revolution in the way we do moral
philosophy and were, historically, probably one of the first calls for
change that would eventually lead to the development of a group of
theories that fall under the term 'virtue ethics'.

Anscombe's paper is well worth reading because of its veritable
revolutionary nature, its passionate and heart-felt arguments against
her perception of the status quo in moral debates and for sowing
some of the seeds that inspired others to revive Aristotelian ideas that
had been largely marginalized up until that time. Her interpretation
is by no means faultless; for example, her characterization of Kantian
theories is far from charitable. Many of her ideas have in turn been
challenged, for example, some contemporary virtue ethicists resist
the apparent conflict between the notions of 'obligation', 'duty' and
'virtue'; however, the paper's main appeal remains in its historical
role in prompting for change. These calls for change characterize this
period in the debate, leading to a growing sense of dissatisfaction
with the state of modern moral philosophy at the time. Thus, many
of the discussions that were the precursors of modern virtue ethics
are about what is wrong with other alternatives, they highlight why
discussions of moral theory have taken a wrong term and prompt
us to redefine the terms of the debate.

The rest of Part I will consider some of these early calls for a
different perspective, the ways in which these early writers sought
to distinguish virtue ethics from other normative theories as well as
some of the repercussions this thinking had for the ways in which
virtue ethics eventually developed into a stand alone, self-contained
alternative to deontology and consequentialism.

2. What do we want from ethics?

A good place to start is to ask what we want from ethical enquiries.
When we think of ethics, most of us think of practical problems:
should I tell my best friend that her partner is cheating on her? Is

it unfair to copy from a friend's essay when I have been too sick to finish my own? Is it permissible for a woman to have an abortion because she is not in a stable relationship and does not want to become a mother? Should higher education be subsidized by the taxpayer for anyone who meets the academic requirements or should Universities be free to charge whatever fees they want in order to attract the students who can afford to pay the most? We expect ethical theories to offer some kind of guidance on how to answer these questions, to help us decide what we should do. This idea is captured in the claim that one of the roles of ethical theories is to be action-guiding, that is, to give us some guidance on what we should do when faced with practical ethical problems.

One of Aristotle's most interesting insights is that he questions the nature of the guidance we should expect from ethical theories. Right at the start of the *Nicomachean Ethics* Aristotle tells us that the book will be an account of ethics and he wonders what kind of answer we should expect from an ethical inquiry. If we are going to be asking ethical questions, what kind of answers should we expect? This is not so much a question about the *content* of the answers, but about what *kind* of answers we should expect to find. Aristotle's response to his own question is that ethics is an imprecise science, so the answer can only be as precise as the subject matter allows, that is in this case, not very precise. If you investigate an imprecise subject matter, you should expect to arrive at an imprecise answer. Ethics involves so much difference and variety that the answers to ethical problems will be diverse and vary both from situation to situation and from person to person. Aristotle warns us: 'Our account of this science [the science of politics; Aristotle seems to understand ethics as the introduction to politics, which in turn he understands as the science of acting morally] will be adequate if it achieves such clarity as the subject-matter allows; for the same degree of precision is not to be expected in all discussions, any more than in all the products of handicraft. Instances of morally fine and just conduct – which is what politics investigates – involve so much difference and variety that they are widely believed to be such only by convention and not by nature'.[1]

It's important to note here that this is not a relativist claim. Relativism is a meta-ethical position which makes certain claims about moral truth, namely that there is no such thing as moral truth. In the same way that there is no truth in matters of taste, there are merely individual preferences (e.g. there is no truth of the matter about whether marmite is objectively tasty or not, it's just that I subjectively hate it and you subjectively love it – both entirely valid, individual responses to a matter of personal taste), there is no truth in moral matters, merely individual preferences. However, this is not Aristotle's claim here. Suggesting that the answer to ethics may be complex, context dependent and difficult to discover is entirely different from claiming that there is no answer. For Aristotle, there is a correct answer to moral matters, but it is complex and not easily captured in a rule, so in this sense, deontologists, consequentialists and Aristotle are all in agreement about the *nature* of moral truth, they all think it's out there! What they disagree about is what kind of *shape* this truth might take.

3. How should I live my life?

Inspired by this Aristotelian insight into the nature of ethics as a discipline and the kind of answer we should expect when discussing topics in ethics, early virtue ethicists suggested that it is a mistake for ethical inquiries to ask 'What should I do?', instead the fundamental questions in ethics should be 'How should I live my life? What kind of person should I be?'.

The first question, 'What should I do?', focuses on a specific situation, what should I do *now*, when faced with *this* problem? It sees ethics as a way of responding to specific, problematic situations. Both deontological and consequentialist theories can be interpreted as attempting to answer this kind of question. Think of the Kantian Categorical Imperative; it is a universal rule that is supposed to give an answer to how we should act when faced with different ethical problems. The Categorical Imperative is a test of proposed maxims, so when faced with an ethical problem we should formulate a proposed course of action, which is captured in the maxim and then the Categorical Imperative gives us an answer as to what we should (or should not) do; similarly is the case with the Utilitarian Greatest Happiness Principle. The Greatest Happiness Principle tells that in all sorts of different situations we should do whatever brings about the greatest happiness for the greatest number of people. As long as we can calculate the expected utility of the consequences of our actions, we can figure out what to do. However, virtue ethicists are worried about this approach as a way of thinking about ethics.

If ethics is an imprecise, varied and diverse subject matter, then one rule or principle cannot be successfully applied to every varied situation we come across, and we cannot expect ethical enquiries to give us concrete answers for specific situations. Consider the following example: take the ethical rule 'Never lie'; this sounds like good advice, it is both helpful, in that it tells you what not to do, and, on the face of it, plausible. Now, consider someone who has decided to follow this rule and is now auditioning to play the role of Romeo for his local amateur theatre group which involves proclaiming his undying love for Juliet. In reality, our actor intensely dislikes the woman playing Juliet, so proclaiming his love for her would be untrue; therefore, he refuses to speak the words as he intends to live his life according to the rule 'Never lie'. This sounds a bit weird, something has gone wrong. Surely acting is pretending within a certain context, that is, a context where both actors and audience are 'in' on the pretence. Under such circumstances, telling Juliet he loves her is not a lie, so our original rule should be modified to explain that acting does not really count as lying.

Having overcome this little hurdle, our aspiring ethicist turns up for his day job as a nurse, where he is asked by a colleague to break some bad news to a patient and 'persuade' the patient to follow a particular course of treatment. The process of persuading the patient involves telling him about only one of two possible treatments and allowing him to believe that this is his only option. Does this count as lying? Our aspiring ethicist has not been asked to utter an untruth, but merely to 'forget' to give all the information, leading the patient to think by his silence that there are no other options. Our aspiring ethicist is now beginning to think that he might be getting himself into trouble; when he first came across his moral rule, 'Never lie', he thought he had succeeded in finding a good guide to being ethical, but now it looks like he will have to stop and consider what counts as lying, how lying relates to other concepts such as 'misleading', 'misdirecting' and 'non-disclosure', which also leads him to wonder about the role of intent in one's expressions.

Our aspiring ethicist heads home feeling that he has taken on more than he bargained for when he decide to follow this one, simple ethical rule, so to take his mind off things he accepts a dinner invitation at his friend's house. His friend, Eddie, has recently divorced his wife and is living on his own for the first time in a very long while. Eddie's confidence in himself and his abilities to cope on his own has been severely tested by the unpleasant divorce and the changes it has led in his life. Our aspiring ethicist is Eddie's first ever dinner guest and Eddie is keen to impress with his new culinary skills and ability to cope on his own. Unfortunately, Eddie is a poor cook and the meal is quite tasteless. When Eddie, enthusiastically, asks our aspiring ethicist 'Did you enjoy the meal?!!!' the aspiring ethicist is stuck. Saying 'yes' would be an outright lie, but surely his friend needs a bit of encouragement and a little lie would not hurt anyone?

You may agree with our aspiring ethicist that his moral rule should be suspended for the moment, or you may not, in a sense it doesn't really matter. What does matter is the realization that if ethics is imprecise, detailed and vague, it cannot be captured in a rigid, universally applicable rule. Our ethicist thought he was onto a winner in the sense that sticking to his rule would give him an answer to what he should do in ethical situations; however, this quickly proved not to be the case. The rule was not sensitive to context, required further thinking in terms of interpreting the term 'lying' and what it involves and did not allow for exceptions such as white lies for the sake of kindness.

4. One size does not fit all

If the purpose of ethical rules is to give us guidance, so that one (or a small set of) overriding rule can give us specific answers to our problems, then it is bound to fail. If ethics is imprecise, then ethical theory cannot hope to offer precise guidance to specific situations as captured in overriding rules. Rules conceived of as all-encompassing, universally applicable, one-size-fits-all solutions to all our ethical problems are not going to work. Rules are far too rigid and prescriptive to ever capture the variety and diversity of ethics. Instead of asking the specific question 'What should I do *here*, *now*, faced with *this* problem?', we should be asking the wider questions 'How should I live my life? What kind of person should I be?' The answer is not going to come in the form of a rule, which once revealed will answer all our ethical problems, but rather in the form of the virtues and the good moral character. We will go on to discuss how the notion of 'character' and the virtues can help us in this way in Chapters 3 and 4 below.

Another way of making the critical point against rules though is to say that ethics is uncodifiable. A code, or set of rules, has many advantages, the principal among which is that it gives clear guidance on what should be done. When in doubt, one simple refers to the code and does as it suggests. Consider the Highway Code which is supposed to serve a similar function, that is, to give road users a set of clear, well defined and easy to both comprehend and apply set of rules by which they can use the roads as safely as possible. The Highway Code has a specific and limited remit and therefore succeeds in giving precise and useful instructions. Even in this case success is not complete and the Courts are called upon to decide on disputed cases, but for the majority of cases appeals to the Highway Code find it provides a clear and incontestable answer. Unfortunately, the same is not true of ethics. This is unfortunate because if ethics could be captured in such a set of clear and incontestable rules, this could potentially resolve most ethical disagreements and provide straightforward guidance in most ethical cases. However, we must not seek easy and fast action guidance at the expense of getting the *right* guidance. For what good is a set of ethical rules if they are precise, quick and easy to apply but wrong?

We can make this same point another way if we consider what is involved in being an expert in a field. If all there is to certain practices is the correct application of rules, the expert is the person who best knows these rules (and by extension applies them as the rules are action guiding). However, expertise is often expressed in knowing when *not* to stick to the rules, in recognizing the instances which are exceptions to the rules, in adjusting to situations that require a novel interpretation of the rules, in creating new rules or in having the reasoning skills to see beyond the rules that capture more common place situations. Consider this account of what it is to be a medical expert:

> If one asks an expert for the rules he or she is using, one will, in effect, force the expert to regress to the level of a beginner and state the rules learned in school. Thus, instead of using rules they no longer remember, as knowledge engineers suppose, the expert is forced to remember rules they no longer use. . .No amount of rules and facts can capture the knowledge an expert has when he or she has stored experience of the actual outcomes of tens of thousands of situations.[2]

The authors conclude that mistakes in deliberation cannot be avoided by attempting to come up with foolproof rules, as there are no such things and this is not what experts rely on when they make their judgements.

There seems to be much more to ethical guidance than practice-focused rules. For example, narratives may play a great role in helping us understand morality; for example, the story of how one friend incurred personal loss to aid another reveals something about the fundamentally other-regarding nature of friendship that can't be captured in a formula prescribing how one should act in each instance of friendship and which is easily transferable as an ideal across many different situations. Or, exercises in empathy, such as asking someone to put themselves in someone else's shoes, may reveal an immediacy to the situation, the impact of which can be otherwise lost.

Furthermore, what is meant by moral notions, such as truthful-ness, cannot be captured in prescriptions about what one should do in any one particular situation. For there is a lot more to truthfulness than the rule 'Always tell the truth'. Someone who truly understands the concept of truthfulness will also understand the nuanced distinctions between lying, misleading and non-disclosure as well as how situations, such as acting or joking, change the tenor of what might otherwise be characterized as a lie. Being truthful doesn't just involve telling the truth, but also being repelled by lies, feeling guilty when one does lie, etc., and in general having the right attitudes and emotions with respect to truth-telling and lying.

Virtue ethics advises us to recognize (and embrace, but we will come to this later) the complexity of the ethical life and accept that the kind of guidance we can expect will have to be tailored to the nature of the subject matter. 'How should I live my life?' is not the kind of question that admits to a quick answer, nor to a simple one, nor to one answer that suits all people and all circumstances, but more on this later on.

Further readings

It's well worth reading Anscombe's original paper, reprinted in Crisp and Slote 1997. Some of the Aristotelian ideas about the nature of ethics and the kind of answers we should expect from ethical inquiry are famously introduced in Book 1 of the *Nicomachean Ethics*. The discussion on the differences between rules and virtues is clearly developed in Roberts, 1991. For more on this topic, you may wish to look up Nussbaum 1986, especially Chapter 10. Themes from Nussbaum's book will also be picked up in Chapter 3 of this volume. See Dancy, 2004, for some of the more recent developments from these kinds of ideas between the juxtaposition of rules and virtues.

CHAPTER TWO

Ethics and morality

1. The limits of morality

Very often when we use the terms 'ethics' and 'morality', we intend them to be used interchangeably to refer to the kinds of considerations that are captured by the 'can, may, should' example above. However, in the discussion that follows, we will use the terms a bit differently to reflect a shift in approach argued for by Bernard Williams, very much in the same spirit as the kinds of considerations that Elizabeth Anscombe brought to the forefront of current debates. Williams was one of the most important philosophers of his generation, partly due to a remarkable philosophical ability: he was often the first person to draw attention to a new problem, a new way of looking at things, a previously neglected distinction, an entirely novel approach. His work often resulted in many of his colleagues picking up his points, either in agreement or in opposition, and establishing entirely new and fruitful areas of debate. These general points apply with much force to his work on morality, which gave rise to many of the ideas that characterize the modern version of virtue ethics, and for this reason it is worth looking at his arguments in a bit more detail.

Partly like Anscombe, Williams was concerned with the notion of 'obligation' and its role within what he called the morality system (in this sense 'morality' here will come to be contrasted with 'ethics', the contrast will become clear in this chapter). This conception of morality is very much influenced by how Williams interpreted

Kantian ethics. He highlighted a number of features of 'obligations' which govern how we understand morality:

1   An obligation applies to someone with respect to an action, it is an obligation to do something (sometimes it may announce a prohibition or a permission that you *may* do something, but it is still action focused), and so morality is practical.

2   Obligations cannot conflict. This is a very important feature of the nature of obligations conceived in this way. What we are obliged to do must be in our power (otherwise being obliged to do it would make no sense), if we are obliged to do more than one thing, then these cannot conflict as it would make it impossible for us to do both.

3   If one has fulfilled all of one's obligations then one can only feel non-moral regret for anything that was not done, since anything that was not done was not an obligation. Under this conception of 'obligation', we need to explain how one consideration outweighs another without generating conflicting obligations (since according to point 2 above, there are no such things as conflicting obligations). One way of doing this is by distinguishing between *prima facie* and actual obligations. In Ross' terminology, a *prima facie* obligation is a moral consideration which has good support for becoming an actual obligation all other things being equal. *Prima facie* obligations exert some force, but not the full force of actual obligations. Consider, for example, a case where you have promised to meet a friend to help him study for an examination. The promise generates a *prima facie* obligation to do as promised. However, on your way to the meeting you are called upon to help in an emergency (make up whatever scenario you want here as long as it means you are the only one who can help, there is no time to both help and fulfil your promise, etc.). The obligation to help in the emergency outweighs the *prima facie* obligation to fulfil your promise. According to Ross, your obligation is to help in the emergency, and there is no conflict of obligations as the promise keeping was not an *actual* obligation in these circumstances but merely a *prima*

facie one. However, at the same time the promise keeping still has some force so you owe your friend reparations for letting him down. This allows Ross to hold that actual obligations cannot conflict (point 2 above) and that what is not done is regrettable (point 3) but not in a strong moral sense as it was not an actual obligation, it was merely a *prima facie* obligation.

4   The fourth point is what Williams calls the 'obligation out-obligation in' principle. Consider this problem: you come across an emergency and you are under the claim 'In this emergency, I am under an obligation to assist', but why is this so? Presumably because 'One is under a general obligation: to help in emergencies', but if we accept such a general obligation it may turn out that *all* our time now is taken up with helping in emergencies and there is no longer any room for any other kind of morally indifferent actions. Since obligations override all other considerations and since here we have an obligation wide enough to occupy all of one's time (unfortunately there are plenty of emergencies around the world), then morality demands that we spend all our time fulfilling its obligations. The only way to 'push out' an obligation is to 'pop another one in', 'obligation out-obligation in', and there is no room for anything else.

5   Since obligations are inescapable, moral blame is the correct response for anyone who did not fulfil their obligations. Once a course of action is established as obligatory, there are no excuses for not pursuing it. This applies to everyone, equally, and there is no perspective from which this is not the case. Both of these claims are seen as fundamental to this conception of Kantian ethics. Consider how they are encapsulated in the Kantian understanding of the Categorical Imperative. The Categorical Imperative is an *imperative* in the sense of a command, it *must* be followed, and it applies *categorically* to everyone, there are no exceptions, no excuses.

These five points then capture the main ways Williams characterizes the notion of 'obligation' and its role in the morality system.

However, he goes on to argue that this particular account of 'obligation' generates a number of problems. For one, trying to understand all moral consideration under the guise of 'obligations' creates more difficulties than it solves. In the promise-keeping example above, all sorts of weird philosophical moves are required to maintain *both* that the *prima facie* obligation can be outweighed by an actual obligation without creating conflict *and* that even though we are not obliged to keep the promise in the face of the emergency, we must still make reparations to the friend for not doing so. If the promise was really outweighed by the emergency, the friend should have nothing to complain about; if it was not, then there were two conflicting obligations, both of which options are a problem for Ross. In real life, Williams argues, it makes much more sense to accept that ethical demands can conflict and deal with the implications of these conflicts (these implications of ethical demands will become clearer throughout this section).

Similarly, this insistence that we can make sense of morality solely through obligations forces all sorts of diverse things into becoming obligations. Williams explains this point by being critical of Ross' 'duties of gratitude'. In an effort to explain gratitude as an obligation, Ross turns what is a sign of good character, that is, the desire to do good to others when we have had good done to us, into an *obligation* to do so. Turning gratitude into an obligation seems to miss the point of what gratitude should really be about. Surely if someone does you a good service, the appropriate response is to be thankful and want to help them out in return when they need you. To make this into an obligation changes the nature of gratitude itself and would make the recipient of the benefit more likely to resent it than be thankful for it. To return a favour out of a sense of duty is quite conceptually different, and relates to the demands of justice, rather than what is involved in returning a favour out of a sense of gratitude. Gratitude involves a positive acknowledgement of the beneficence illustrated in the benefactor's act and a desire to reciprocate. The reciprocation need not always be direct, one may express one's gratitude by conferring a suitable benefit to a third party and not directly back to the original benefactor; for example, I am grateful that someone helped me find an apartment and a job when I was homeless, so now I return the favour by helping other homeless people do the same. This still counts as gratitude as it embodies and promotes the sentiments and values of the original benefactor. To label all this an obligation is to miss the point of real gratitude because an obligation involves doing something out of sense of duty and unavoidability rather than because one is happy to receive the benefit and happy to conceive of oneself as someone who has been benefited by the benefactor. Ethical demands are much wider than moral obligations, and we want our theory to make room for, and sense of, all these diverse demands rather than attempting to awkwardly reduce everything to obligations.

Another implication of this view of obligations is that only an obligation can beat an obligation. This turns almost everything into an obligation, causing the types of problems highlighted just above, but it also leaves little or no room for morally indifferent actions. We would actually need to come up with obligations to explain why we should be allowed to do morally indifferent actions, because if they are not obligations, then we should not be wasting time on them. This leads to a life dominated by obligations with little or no room for anything else. Again Williams' conception of ethics is much wider than his account of morality here. As we shall come to see, the ethical life involves many other commitments, commitments which we can make sense of under this wider conception of ethics, but not the narrow conception of morality. Ethics allows us to make room for the idea 'that each person has a life to lead',[1] a life which should not be overwhelmed by moral obligations, but which allows room for other considerations that make one's life meaningful.

Finally we do not need to accept that every obligation comes from a more general obligation. A better way to understand what is happening in positive cases, cases regarding what we should do, is that there is a general underlying concern or disposition, for example, a disposition to help others in need, but that this disposition does not always outweigh everything else. Rather, it can become a deliberative priority (what we actually do) because of the particulars of the situation we are faced with now. Some situations will activate our concerns and dispositions, others will not, without having to rely on the 'obligation out-obligation in' principle. We will discuss how general dispositions become deliberative priorities because of the particulars of situations when we look at the Aristotelian concepts of 'moral perception' and 'practical wisdom' later on in Chapter 5.

Williams' understanding of 'morality' then turns out to be rather different from that of 'ethics'. The morality system is dominated by this particular notion of 'obligation', while ethics allows room for more diverse considerations. This allows ethics to give a more plausible account of phenomena such as gratitude, which morality is forced into distorting in order to make them comprehensible through the notion of 'obligation', as well as allowing for a wider concept of what counts as a meaningful life for human beings. Morality gets into problems by denying the possibility of conflicting obligations and reduces all obligations to more general ones, while ethics allows room for conflict and gives a different account of how some claims become deliberative priorities. These concerns with this particular conception of 'obligation' and its dominance over what Williams calls the 'morality system' lead him to call for a number of revisions, which we will consider below. The next chapter will further develop the final arguments in Williams' discussion which have to do with his rejection of an account of voluntariness that leaves no room for character and psychological or social determination, his rejection of the purity of morality and his rejection of the idea that morality transcends luck – but we can set these thoughts aside for now as we first need to consider what is involved in living a meaningful life. In looking at all these ideas that are, in a broad sense, inspired by Williams, we will now move away from Williams' own work and consider how these themes were taken up by other authors.

2. The meaningful life

What is involved in living a meaningful life? In what sense is the above conception of ethics broader than that of morality and how does it allow room for wider considerations that make our lives meaningful? Consider the following scenario: the boat you were on has capsized, there are no other adults around or any promise of immediate help, unfortunately there are two babies drowning near you but in entirely different directions so that you only have time to rescue one of them before the other one drowns. Although no one baby is closer to you than the other, one is the baby of a stranger, the other is your baby – which one would you chose to save? I would imagine many people would want to save their own child at the expense of the stranger's child and would want to do so exactly because this is their *own* child, but is this the right thing to do?

In one sense, impartiality is conceptually tied to morality, in that to treat people partially is to treat them unfairly, or unduly promote or penalize them, and this seems incompatible with moral demands. Surely, morality requires of us to treat all others equally and to allow our personal preferences and prejudices to affect our choices is not compatible with doing the right thing. However, this account of the importance of impartiality is also question begging because treating people impartially does not mean that we should give them exactly *the same* treatment, rather that we should allocate different treatments on a warranted basis – deciding which differences are warranted is the crux of the matter. Suppose you had to mark a number of essays and your marks were critical to the chances of the students passing their exams and therefore obtaining their degrees – clearly a serious task which you wish to undertake with all due responsibility. The submitted essays differ in a variety of ways, some are handwritten, some are word-processed, some are typed in Times New Roman font, some in Arial, some are printed in black ink, some are printed in blue ink, etc. Your task is to decide which ones of these differences are pertinent to awarding different marks. Should all handwritten essays pass, while all word-processed ones fail? Should all students who chose to type in Times New Roman get a first-class mark, while all Arial users barely a third? By now you should, hopefully, be perplexed by my choice of highlighted differences! Surely, this is a bizarre course that measures academic ability based on factors as random and irrelevant as choice of typescript, choice of ink colour, etc. This worry reveals that when we are called upon to differentiate between different demands, we should do so on criteria appropriate to the task. If these are philosophy essays, then you would be warranted in awarding high marks to all essays that achieve a high level of clarity, analysis, exposition, critical and independent thinking, and by extension a low mark to all essays that are unclear, confused, uninformed and overtly descriptive. These criteria are not random, like the typescript and ink colour selections, precisely because they relate to the nature of the enterprise under examination. Philosophy concerns itself with clear, original, persuasive arguments, so it is appropriate that essays that demonstrate good philosophical skills should be rewarded in a task which involves the evaluation of philosophical skills.

What this example demonstrates is that how we treat others and whether our treatment is warranted or not depends on what is being assessed and on the strength of the various claims placed upon us, something which is relative to the task undertaken. When Aristotle tells us that justice is to be found in treating equals equally, he gives us both an important and challenging insight. The insight is important as it captures the link between justice and morality, and challenging because we are still left with the difficult job of giving content to what counts as 'being equal'.

Let's go back to the example of the drowning babies and see how all this applies to that case. Hopefully, we can all agree that we have equal obligations to save equally threatened babies; however, what counts as an equally warranted claim for rescue on us, given that we can only save one baby at the expense of another? A consequentialist might conclude that the stranger's baby has an equal claim to that of your own baby, as the evaluation of the claims is based on the interests of the babies. *Any* drowning baby will experience the same pain and suffering through the drowning, *any* drowning baby's future interests will be equally severed by its premature drowning; therefore, the fact that one baby is yours while the other is not is entirely irrelevant to the question of which baby to save in the same way that the typescript choice was irrelevant to the quality of the essay above. Equal interests generate equal claims, so the stranger's baby has as much of a claim of rescue on you, as your own baby and the fact that you are biologically related to one of the babies in need is irrelevant here.

Virtue ethicists have found this type of reasoning problematic, partly because it gives a distorted account of what impartiality requires of us and partly because it results in a very poor conception of what makes a human life meaningful. The first point has to do with the interpretation of the factors we are allowed to take into account when deciding between competing claims. Why can't a parent's special feelings towards their own children be allowed to count as a factor in favour of saving *that* child, in the same way that exceptional clarity of argument counts in favour of awarding a high mark to this particular philosophy essay? The parent's feelings are a distinguishing feature of the situation, one which differentiates between the two babies in need of rescue, why should it not be accepted as a warranted feature? The second point concerns the idea that if we do away with all these considerations, if we distance ourselves from our special feelings towards our children, if we ignore the unique demands of our friends, if we alienate ourselves from all the important relationships in our lives which make some people stand out above others, we would be depriving our lives of much of their meaning. Surely, we can come up with a conception of ethics that accommodates all these relationships and allows us to lead meaningful lives compatible with living good lives. In this sense, we can be partial, we can allocate special weight to special relationships, but this partiality is warranted and we are still treating equals equally as the criteria on which we determine equality are defensible and justified.

Despite the existence of a significant number of University campuses with lakes, the observant reader may worry here that the chances of having to rescue equidistant drowning babies from the aforementioned lakes are rather slim, at least for most of us. However, we shouldn't allow the improbability of this particular example to shadow the importance of the point it is trying to make. That is because fundamentally the example is about the significance of family, friendships and other special relationships in our life and the claim that awarding special status to these relationships is not contrary to morality, but rather a fundamental part of leading a meaningful life. We are not all called upon to save drowning babies, but we are all called upon to consider how our behaviour towards those near and dear to us might differ from our other behaviour towards strangers. To attempt to eliminate such differences would not only impose an unreasonable burden on us but also leads to much poorer, duller lives.

3. Why you don't want to be a moral saint

If you have children or if you ever think about what kind of people you would like your future children to become, you probably hope you can raise them to be moral people, people who chose to do the right thing. However, would you want to go as far as hoping that they would be moral saints, people whose every action is as good as possible? If being morally good is something to aspire to, then it seems to follow that being *perfectly* morally good would be even better. Surprisingly though, this is not the case.

Think for a moment about what kind of person the moral saint would be. She would pursue the happiness of others, either because her happiness consisted in bringing about the happiness of others or because her duty consisted in bringing about the happiness of others. These moral demands would 'crowd-out' all sorts of other non-moral activities, like the pursuit of intellectual and aesthetic pleasures, so no University studies or gallery visits for our moral saint; like the enjoyment of material comforts, so no back massages or sophisticated cuisine for our moral saint; like the pleasures involved in spending time with those we love, so no family reunions and no time wasted going bowling with friends for our moral saint – a rather one-sided, single-focused life. At the same time, some attitudes seem incompatible with being a moral saint. A sarcastic wit requires a pessimistic attitude to the world which is incompatible with the positive attitude required of the moral saint. In Eudenides' novel *The Marriage Plot* one of the main characters is contemplating a life devoted to charity and good deeds. While helping out at a hospital run by Mother Teresa in India, he observes how boring and dull his fellow volunteers are; he wonders: 'What if you had faith and performed good works, what if you died and went to heaven, what if all the people you met there were people you didn't like?'[2] Our moral saint could well end up being a rather dull and humourless person. All in all, the life of the moral saint doesn't quite sound like the life one would want for oneself or would hope for, for one's children.

The problem is that it looks like consequentialism and deontology counsel us to attempt to live the lives of moral saints. Being good is, under these theories, not just one desire among many, or even one that overwhelms all our other desires, like the committed athlete who sacrifices nights out and fun with friends in favour of daily training. Rather, the desire to be morally good, and as morally good as possible, will subsume and demote all other desires so that they are entirely lost. Again, we have a conception of morality here as an imperative, whose command is different from the nature of every other motivation. If there is any value in other activities, it is only through the prism of morality, so the Utilitarian might accord equal weight to his own happiness, but as only one the many equal requirements placed on him and as just one requirement it is likely to be outweighed by the multiple demands of others. All the non-moral activities mentioned above only have value as means to producing happiness and can be exchanged with other activities which produce an equal or greater amount of happiness. Similarly, deontologists only value these activities insofar as they encapsulate respect for the moral law. However, this leads to both a poor and less fulfilled life and misunderstands the value of non-moral activities.

4. How to avoid moral schizophrenia

This may come as a bit of a surprise to you but being moral is a dangerous business. You are in danger of succumbing to moral schizophrenia:

> One mark of the good life is a harmony between one's motives and one's reasons, values, justifications. Not to be moved by what one values – what one believes good, nice, right, beautiful, and so on – bespeaks a malady of the spirit. Not to value what moves one also bespeaks a malady of the spirit. Such a malady, or such maladies, can properly be called *moral schizophrenia* – for they are a split between one's motives and one's reasons.[3]

A Utilitarian may well find a place for friendship, family relationships, community bonds, etc. in his theory, but will do so only insofar as they go towards promoting general happiness. These activities, these commitments, are therefore not valued for themselves, but rather for what they lead to, for the kinds of consequences they bring about. The *reason* a Utilitarian has for promoting friendship is to bring about good consequences, but surely this is not the usual motive we all have for engaging in friendships. We don't seek out new friends because we are motivated to increase overall utility, rather we are motivated by the friendship itself, something which is intrinsic to the relationship itself rather than a possible by-product of it.

Here's another way of making the same point. Imagine you are in hospital feeling a bit poorly and your best friend pops by. Cheered by her visit you thank her for taking the time to come see you and she replies 'No worries, just doing my duty'. Now that seems a bit odd, and even worse, a bit off-putting. Had she said 'No worries, that's what friends are for' you would have been quite pleased and taken the explanation at face value. That's because *that is* what friends are for, they are suppose to care for each other, check up on each other in times of need, be attentive and kind; all this just *is* part of friendship and appealing to the friendship is explanation enough for why she is visiting. By contrast, appealing to a notion of duty might make you feel resentful of the visit and you may even wish she hadn't bothered. She's not supposed to come see you because she *had* to, because she felt *obliged* to do so, but because she *wanted* to and the explanation for why she wanted to is simply captured by stating that she is your friend. By appealing to her duty to visit you, your friend is having 'one thought too many', a phrase coined by Bernard Williams to explain the idea that appealing to friendship alone is sufficient without the need to understand the demands of friendship through the prism of duty, and this appeal to friendship is more than sufficient; it's satisfactory all by itself in a way that appealing to the extra thought about one's duty is not necessary. We want our friends to come see us *because* they are our friends, not because they feel obliged to do so and the bonds of friendship should not be felt as restraints or commands.

The hospital example makes the same point regarding a split, a disharmony, schizophrenia between reasons and motives, but this time applies it to our other, by now familiar, opponent, the deontologist. The charge then applies equally to both consequentialists and deontologists; their theories lead to a split between what we have reason to do and what we are motivated to do. By carrying out the relationship for the sake of the good consequences or out of a sense of duty, one misses out the essential element of friendship which is the commitment to the activity and to the friend. If the resulting goodness is all that matters, friends would be interchangeable and indeed one would be obliged to drop one friend as soon as another came along who had more potential for producing good consequences. Friendship only makes sense by reference to the specific relationship, to the ties that bind the two friends, by relating to the friend as the kind of person he is and for the sake of who he really is. To aim at friendship in general as a good to be maximized or a duty to be fulfilled, misses the point of actual friendship.

Following the dictates of consequentialism and deontology leads to two problems. What kind of life would I lead if I did my duty but rarely wanted to, that is, if my reasons and motives were in disharmony? Surely, this cannot be what we want as a worthwhile and meaningful life for human beings. Second, the exaggerated focus on notions of obligation and rightness leads us to ignore or distort all sorts of other values like interpersonal activities and narrows the sphere of what we should consider important.

As we reach the end of this chapter, we have seen the same pattern of reasoning laid out by a variety of authors in a number of different ways, but essentially the point is the same. Morality is pre-occupied with a particular conception of obligation which is both restrictive and distorting. It either ignores or subsumes all sorts of other values under this conception of obligation, leading to a very poor conception of what counts as a meaningful life. It also distorts what these values are really about, mistakenly thinking that they can all be understood under a legislative model of reasoning. What we need therefore is a new perspective, a wider perspective, one that asks what is the good life for me to lead – an ethical question rather than a moral one – and one which can accommodate a variety of human concerns as well as the moral ones.

Further readings

The ideas discussed in this chapter are developed at length in Williams, 1985. Have a look at other works by Williams for further discussions, for example, Williams, 1973, on the practical nature of morality and the impossibility of obligations conflicting, Williams, 1981a on agent regret (themes from this paper will be further developed in Chapter 3 of this volume) and his 1981b on the 'one thought too many' objection. The Stanford Encyclopaedia of Philosophy entry on Bernard Williams is particularly helpful.

You can read Ross's original ideas on *prima facie* obligations (or 'duties' in his terminology), in Ross, 1931. Modern Kantians make a similar point with *pro tanto* reasons, see, for example, Kagan, 1989.

For Aristotle's thoughts on justice, see Book V of the *Nicomachean Ethics*.

Modern authors who take up Williams' calls for change include Cottingham, in Crisp, 1996, for a defence and elaboration of the notion of partiality, Wolf's seminal 1982 and Stocker's influential, 1976.

CHAPTER THREE

Character and the emotions

1. The purity of morality

We can now move on to another important aspect of the virtue ethical critique of the status quo as exemplified by consequentialist and deontological theories, namely their neglect of the important role moral character should play in ethical theories. The notion of 'character' in virtue ethics is a technical one, and we will consider below how virtue ethicists understand it, but first we need to discuss the critique of theories which disregard the importance of character. In order to do this, we have to return to the work of Bernard Williams.

A dominant idea driving much of Kant's thought, especially in the *Groundwork of the Metaphysics of Morals*, is what Williams calls the 'purity of morality'. Kant begins the *Groundwork* by establishing that the supreme principle of morality, what the work is aiming to establish, must be unconditionally good. It cannot be grounded either in the dictates of God or in a teleological conception of human nature (i.e. the idea that human nature has a function, a goal, an end) or in utility, as any of these options would make morality conditional by grounding it in something else. The only thing which is good unconditionally, without qualification, without relying on other things for its goodness, is the good will. And that means that the goodness of the good will is not affected by things such as consequences, results, ulterior ends, compulsion, fame, happiness and pleasure. In a famous passage Kant writes:

> Even if, by some special disfavour of destiny or by the niggardly endowment of step-motherly nature, this will is entirely lacking in power to carry out its intentions; if by its utmost effort it still accomplishes nothing, and only good will is left (not admittedly, as a mere wish, but as the straining of every means so far as they are in our control); even then it would still shine like a jewel for its own sake as something which has its full value in itself.[1]

If the will were to be prevented from carrying out its purpose, either by 'some special disfavour of destiny' or by 'the niggardly endowment of step-motherly nature', it would still remain pure and good. The 'special disfavour of destiny' is simply a misfortune, you want to save the drowning baby but unfortunately she is too far away from you to reach in time. So bad luck and bad circumstances can stop you from achieving the good result, but, importantly, this has no bearing on the goodness of the good will. The good will remains good even if it fails in bringing about any good consequences. The 'niggardly endowment of step-motherly nature' means a contrary natural characteristic. So if you have the will to act, but you are prevented from doing so by your own temperament, that is, your own nature, your will is still good and you are good. So if your will prescribes saving the baby, but you are naturally lazy or cruel so you don't, you are still good by virtue of your good will. It is this second idea that interests us here, the idea that the goodness of the good will is entirely independent of natural dispositions, emotions and other factors that go towards shaping who we become. It is this conception of morality as pure that Williams objects to when he rejects the Kantian morality's pressure to

> . . . require a voluntariness that will be total and will cut through character and psychological or social determination, and allocate blame and responsibility on the ultimately fair basis of the agent's own contribution, no more no less. It is an illusion to suppose that this demand can be met.[2]

The Kantian rejection of emotional and social influences on the good will comes from a mistrust of these influences and their arbitrary and uncontrollable nature. For Kant, human beings are imperfectly rational beings because we are influenced by two sources of motivation, reason and desire. If we were motivated purely by reason, we would be perfectly rational beings and we would always will what is rational, that is, what is moral. We are not though, we are imperfectly rational beings; this does not mean that we do not know what is rational or moral, but rather that we do not always will it because of our desires. Desires are subversive, they are given to us by nature without us having any choice in the matter, for example, some people are born naturally kind, even tempered and courageous, while others are born naturally cruel, irascible and cowardly, also without having any choice in these natural tendencies. Furthermore, our desires develop and are influenced by external factors such as social influences over which we have no control whatsoever. Since we have no control over our desires, we are not masters of our own selves in this respect and desires cannot be the foundation of morality. A fundamental aspect of morality is that we praise and blame people for their moral actions and this in turn requires that they have control over what they choose to do – the notion of 'voluntariness'. If all morality comes down to is external influences and uncontrollable desires, we would never be able to hold anyone morally responsible for anything they did. One's motives then are crucial for Kant.

In another often quoted passage from the *Groundwork*, Kant expands on this point:

> To be beneficent where one can is a duty, and besides there are many souls so sympathetically attuned that, without any other motive of vanity or self-interest they find an inner satisfaction in spreading joy around them and can take delight in the satisfaction of others so far as it is in their own work. But I assert that in such a case an action of this kind, however it may conform with duty and however amiable it may be, has nevertheless no true moral worth but is on the same footing with other inclinations, for example, the inclination to honor, which, if it fortunately lights upon what is in fact in the common interest and in conformity with duty and hence honourable, deserves praise and encouragement but not esteem; for the maxim lacks moral content, namely that of doing such actions not from inclination but *from duty*. Suppose then that the mind of this friend of man

were overclouded by sorrows of his own which extinguished all
sympathy with the fate of others, but that he still had the power
to help those in distress, though no longer stirred by the need of
others because sufficiently occupied with his own; and suppose
that. when no longer moved by an inclination, he tears himself
out of this deadly insensibility and does the action without any
inclination for the sake of duty alone; then for the first time
his action has genuine moral worth. Still further: if nature had
implanted little sympathy in this or that man's heart; if . . . he
were cold in temperament and indifferent to the sufferings of
others – perhaps because, being endowed with the special gift of
patience and robust endurance in his own sufferings, he assumed
the like in others or even demanded it; if such a man (who would
in truth not be the worst product of nature) were not exactly
fashioned by her to be a philanthropist, would he not still find in
himself a source from which he might draw a worth far higher
than any that a good-natured temperament can have?[3]

The second man in this passage has true moral worth, as he acts out
of duty, he acts because he reasons that it is his duty to do so, and
this is independent of any incidental desires he may have. In this
case, it is even contrary to the incidentally unhelpful desires that
he happens to have. The first man acts well but it is a coincidence
that he does so, as he does so merely because he happens to have
sympathetic tendencies which he is neither responsible for nor
able to control. The problem with the first man is that his actions
are conditional on desires which may at any moment wane and
disappear, and his actions would disappear with them. The first
man is at best due our encouragement as what he does is at least
in accordance with duty (even if this accordance is incidental), but
never our moral esteem as that is only due to those who act from
the pure motive of duty.

The Kantian picture then is one where the emotions are irrelevant
to moral worth and moral praise and blame are 'pure' in the sense
that they are divorced from natural inclinations, psychological
factors, social influences, etc. For virtue ethicists, this entire picture
is incorrect and distorts both the proper understanding of the
relationship between reason and the emotions and the proper role
of character in moral theory.

2. The notion of 'character'

The Kantian picture of morality allows us to make pure judgements of responsibility, that is, when we hold someone morally praise or blameworthy, we have a specific conception of voluntariness in mind, one which is free from external influences, social factors, psychological impulses, the emotions, etc. However, this purity is attained at the cost of plausibility. Even a cursory look at human behaviour shows that if we abstract all kinds of emotional reactions and social influences from the moral sphere, we end up with an implausible and unsatisfactory account. To correct this, we need to reconsider how we should make moral judgements grounded on a theory of character.

The notion of 'character' employed here is a technical one, so it's worth taking a bit of time to explore what it means. The etymology of the term comes from the Greek for carving or engraving, a process for making a distinctive and durable mark and this tells us something about our understanding of character. One's character is distinctive, it refers to qualities that make that particular person who they are. Indeed, we sometimes use the term 'character' to capture this very notion of distinctiveness, for example, as in when we call a TV reality show participant 'quite a character' to intimate that they stand out, that they are memorable, that they are different from others. Asking for an account of someone's character involves asking for an account of the ways in which they stand out from other people, the ways in which their beliefs, attitudes and subsequent actions differentiate them from other people.

Distinctiveness is a characteristic that the term 'character' also shares with the notion of 'personality', but at the same time, character goes beyond the notion of distinctiveness. Learning about a person's character tells us something about who they are, in the sense of revealing their commitments, what they consider important, the attitudes and behaviours that person counts as identifying of his or her own self and his or her own agency. Our character is, in many ways, indicative of who we are. And since many of our most important commitments are moral commitments, many aspects of our character have to do with our moral attitudes and behaviours. While one's sense of who one is will involve all sorts of factors outside of one's character, for example, one's age, gender, occupation, etc., it will also partly involve what we believe in, what we are committed to, what we value, what we are interested in, etc., all of which are aspects of our characters. We should also note that these values and commitments need not concern extraordinary or rare occurrences but, more likely, will be about everyday concerns and responsibilities.

Thinking about our commitments and values reveals another aspect of character, and this is its stability. Moral commitments are serious commitments, in the sense that they are only undertaken after a lot of reflection and once undertaken they are persistent and show a high degree of steadfastness. If you, on reflection, decide that kindness to others is a value you should pursue, encourage and dedicate yourself to, then you are likely to be strongly committed to being kind, a commitment which will persist over time and manifest itself reliably in a variety of different situations. You are unlikely to suddenly decide to give cruelty a go simply on a whim, or because you have nothing better to do or because you didn't really think about it. One's stable character traits not only will capture who we are but also will do so persistently over time, showing a level of commitment appropriate to the gravity of the activity. In this sense, one's character is very much like a permanent engraving, deeply etched, difficult to erase and persistent over time.

Now, one might object here that people's characters change all the time, after all we are often surprised on revisiting old friends by seeing how different they are to our earlier memories, we expect children to mature into more complex and sophisticated persons as adults, we see character change as a necessary and central part of moral maturity. However, these two ideas, the idea of stability and the idea of change need not be contradictory; they may just refer to different stages of character development. Much of our lives may well be spent on trying to discover who we really are, on thinking about what kinds of values we should commit ourselves to, on testing our abilities to react to different situations, on learning, growing and improving ourselves. At the same time, once we have committed ourselves to certain characteristic modes of attitude and behaviour, they are likely to display a pattern of reliability and stability. The *process* of character formation may be gradual, subject to change, experimentation and discovery, the *settled state* of one's character is stable, dependable and predictable.

3. Character development

Given the claims above, how we come to develop our characters, the process by which we become who we are, is going to be very significant for our discussion. It seems to be true that we are all born with all sorts of different natural tendencies. If we look at even very young children, we can observe differences between them; some are more irascible, others are more settled in temperament, some are more sociable, others are happier on their own, some are more willing to share, others are more possessive, etc. It is reasonable to assume then that those who are fortunate enough to be born with a preponderance of positive tendencies will find it easier to cultivate a good character, whereas those who are born with a preponderance of negative tendencies will have more obstacles to overcome. Aristotle writes:

> Some thinkers hold that it is by nature that people become good, others that it is by habit, and others that it is by instruction. The bounty of nature is clearly beyond our control; it is bestowed by some divine dispensation upon those who are truly fortunate. It is a regrettable fact that discussion and instruction are not effective in all cases; just as a piece of land has to be prepared beforehand if it is to nourish the seed, so the mind of the pupil has to be prepared in his habits if it is to enjoy and dislike the right things; because the man who lives in accordance with his feelings would not listen to an argument to dissuade him, or understand it if he did. And when a man is in that state, how is it possible to persuade him out of it? In general, feeling seems to yield not to argument but only to force. Therefore we must have a character to work on that has some affinity to virtue: one that appreciates what is noble and objects to what is base.[4]

Kant and Aristotle would both agree that we are born with good or bad natural tendencies, over which we have no control, but which can shape the way we develop and eventually the way we behave; however, they disagree over how we should react to this fact. For Kant, we should aim to expunge the influence of uncontrollable natural impulses for they pollute the purity of morality. For Aristotle, we should recognize and embrace their influence.

We embrace the influence of natural tendencies by encouraging and promoting those that are good, while discouraging and minimizing the effect of those that are bad. The most important point to note about Aristotelian character development is that it is a long, gradual process which involves different stages (not just stages of progress but also regression and deterioration and not only wholesale change but also partial change in some areas rather than others) in both cognitive and affective aspects of our character. Not only do we start with natural tendencies that may influence us in good or bad ways but we also develop due to external factors which may also influence us in good or bad ways. To understand this process of gradual development, we need to consider the move from knowing 'the that' to understanding 'the because' (these are Burnyeat's very useful translations of the original Aristotelian terms).

The process of moral character development starts with finding out 'the that'. 'The that' is the right thing to do, but we learn what that might be through example, habituation, external influences and so on. Consider a child that refuses to share his toys with other children. His father intervenes and says something like 'It's good to share your toys with other children who have none'. At this stage, the child has learnt something about morality, but what it has learnt is limited. The lesson has to do with the content of morality as applied to this example, but importantly the child has yet to learn why it is good to share, when it might be acceptable not to share and it has not internalized the values exemplified by sharing in such a way that the child himself comes to affirm the importance of sharing as one of his values. All this will come in time with further development, but to start off, we are dependent on seeing and following the example of others who know better. In this respect, it makes all the difference whether we have good role models, good parents, good friends and good influences which will steer us towards the good, even if we don't yet fully understand the good ourselves.

> A wide range of desires and feelings are shaping patterns of motivation and response in a person well before he comes to a reasoned outlook on his life as a whole, and certainly before he integrates this reflective consciousness with his actual behaviour.[5]

Because of such external influences, how we behave now has a great role to play in shaping who we will become. Aristotle counsels us to become just by performing just acts,[6] which at first glance sounds circular. For how can we perform just acts without knowing what they are, and how will we know what they are before we have become just? The answer to this conundrum is to be found in two different understandings of what it is to perform just acts. One can perform just acts because one is counselled to do so – this person knows 'the that', what to do – but one can only be truly just when one understands 'the because', that is, why the act is just, exactly what is required by justice, why acting justly is important and along with this comes an internalization of the value of justice such that one comes to affirm the value of justice. We move from a belief that we should do something because it is just, a belief that has been instilled in us by the good example of others, to an understanding of why it is so that comes with a personal commitment to doing what is just *because* it is just.

This process of development from believing 'the that' to understanding 'the because' involves both cognitive and affective elements. It is not sufficient to merely have an intellectual understanding of kindness, one must also develop one's affective responses to function in a kind way. The kind person doesn't just merely think kind thoughts, he has kind feelings and more importantly than that, it is the connection of both kind thoughts and feelings that lead to kind actions. Habit is crucial in developing the right emotions, for it is in habituating ourselves to act and feel in particular ways that we actually come to act and feel in these ways for real. It is important to note though that virtue is not habit. Habits are unreflective, routine behaviours and having the right habits helps us to develop the right dispositions, but true virtue requires conscious choice and choosing virtue for its own sake. Therefore, virtue cannot be habit, although habit is a useful tool towards establishing the right emotional responses and first reactions.

We will return to the importance of developing the right emotional responses in the next part of this volume, but for now it is sufficient to note that character development will be as much about developing the right feelings as it will be about developing the right ways of thinking. Full understanding of 'the because' is not merely a rational matter, it is also a matter of being moved in the right way. Again from Aristotle:

> It is the way that we behave in our dealings with other people that makes us just or unjust, and the way that we behave in the face of danger, accustoming ourselves to be timid or confident, that makes us brave or cowardly. Similarly with situations involving desires and angry feelings: some people become temperate and patient from one kind of conduct in such situations, others licentious and choleric from another. In a word, then, like activities produce like dispositions. Hence we must give our activities a certain quality, because it is their characteristics that determine the resulting dispositions. So it is a matter of no little importance what sorts of habits we form from the earliest age – it makes a vast difference, or rather all the difference in the world.[7]

This is how we move from natural tendencies, through the influence of external factors, to settled dispositions.

Finally, one last aspect of character is its link with action. Character is a state of being expressed in doing. It is a state of being that involves evolving or settled dispositions with both cognitive and affective elements that flow into appropriate action. To have a kind character is to be disposed to act in kind ways where kindness is what is required, and similarly with other dispositions. In this respect, character-based theories are different from both consequentialist theories that focus on the importance of the results of one's actions and deontological theories that focus on the importance of the motives behind our actions. Character theories are interested in both the beliefs and desires that shape our dispositions and the actions that proceed from those dispositions. Of course, this doesn't mean that all dispositions result in actions all of the time, but we will leave the topics of acting out of character and the possibility of our being prevented from realizing our dispositions in action until Chapter 7.

4. The fragility of goodness

The Aristotelian picture of character development then has the advantage of plausibility over the Kantian aspiration to a pure morality. Within this account, we can make sense of the importance of the raw materials we are born with and the numerous external influences we are subjected to during our lives. However, one possible objection here is that plausibility is gained at the cost of injustice. The Kantian pure morality goes hand in hand with a particular understanding of justice in making moral judgements. If the possibility to choose morality is open to anyone at any time, regardless of background or influences, at least there is a sense of justice in holding people morally responsible as we are holding them morally responsible for something they chose to do. In the Aristotelian picture by contrast, one's character is subject to all these uncontrollable influences, so how can we hold people responsible for what they become and what they do if they didn't have full control over their character's formation in the first place?

Consider two children of similar age. Sophie is born with some disadvantageous natural qualities; she has a tendency to irascibility, a rather self-centred approach to life and an inflated sense of her own self importance. She is born to a family of poor means, living in a deprived area, with few educational and cultural opportunities. Her father is not present in her life and her mother suffers from substance abuse problems. Her school is poorly funded, has difficulty in recruiting top-rated teachers and has a high truancy rate. Sophie's friends are likely to be involved in petty crimes at a young age, possible substance abuse later on and many of her friends give up on their education at a young age. By contrast, July is born with some advantageous natural qualities, she has a natural tendency to kindness; she is even-tempered and generous. She is born to a cultured and well-educated family, who has educational aspirations for her and the financial means to support a private education, trips abroad, visits to cultural sites, etc. Her friends all come from similar backgrounds and have plans to pursue higher education and rewarding careers. It would be no surprise if Sophie's life took a completely different turn from July's life, but given the disparities in both natural tendencies and background influences it does seem unfair to blame Sophie and praise July for characters whose formation was predominantly out of their control. Of course, neither Sophie's nor July's paths are predestined, and we would be full of admiration for Sophie if she were to break through the constraints of her upbringing, but if she were to do so, she would be the exception rather than the rule.

It is these kinds of considerations that have led some philosophers to worry that the Aristotelian picture of moral development is both elitist and unfair. Under this picture, morality is the privilege of the few, those who have had the good luck to have support and encouragement but also the finances and means to become moral. This kind of worry has led some commentators to very harsh criticisms of Aristotle; here is Bertrand Russell on the topic:

> The book [the *Nicomachean Ethics*] appeals to the respectable middle-aged, and has been used by them, especially since the seventeenth century, to repress the ardours and enthusiasms of the young. But to a man with any depth of feeling it is likely to be repulsive.[8]

This is a serious concern, and it is important to see whether it can be rebuffed.

Essentially, the Aristotelian response will follow lines of argument similar to the ones we have considered above, when discussing the nature of ethics. If the nature of ethics is such that it is vulnerable to luck and uncontrollable contingencies, then this is not the fault of the ethical theory that seeks to describe and account for these ideas. To deny that this is so is to create an unrealistic picture of ethics which doesn't serve in helping us understand what kinds of persons we should aim to become. In the same way that we mustn't seek a precise and rule-bound answer for a diverse and context sensitive topic, we mustn't seek an answer free from the influences of luck for an enterprise that is fundamentally vulnerable to luck. If the influence of luck is part of ethics, then our ethical theory needs to take this into account, rather than blindly deny it. As we shall come to see in Part II, the good human life is fragile in many different respects; it is not just the vulnerability of character development but also the requirement of external goods such as friendship which are both central to living the good life but also difficult to find and maintain, as well as the possibility of falling foul of great disasters that upset all of one's projects. In the next three chapters we'll see how recognizing and accepting the fragility of goodness is not only a requirement of giving a plausible account of ethics but also an advantage, something we should welcome and embrace, for it is only that which is vulnerable and difficult to achieve that is also precious and worth pursuing.

Further readings

Kant's thoughts discussed in this chapter can be found in the first part of the *Groundwork of the Metaphysics of Morals*. Williams' critique of the Kantian pure morality is developed in Williams, 1985.

The ideas discussed in the sections on character development are very much based on Aristotle's thoughts from Book II of the *Nicomachean Ethics*. There are a number of useful discussions of the notion of character as relating to virtue ethics, for example, Kupperman, 1991, especially Chapters 1, 2 and 3, or for a very clearly presented account of these ideas, see Annas, 2011, Chapters 2 and 3. One of the most excellent discussions of the process of character formation is Burnyeat, in Rorty, 1980.

Bertrand Russell's damning account of Aristotle's ethics can be found in Russell, 1946 and is worth reading as his interpretation of Aristotle was very influential for a long time. Martha Nussbaum's response is one of the most eloquent and moving accounts of Aristotelian ethics available, Nussbaum, 1986, Chapter 11, although most of these ideas will be covered in Part II when we discuss the link between *eudaimonia* and virtue.

Conclusion for Part One

In this first part of this volume, we have covered a very wide number of ideas. If you are interested in pursuing any of them further, the 'Further Readings' section at the end of each chapter lets you know about the authors who discussed and defended these ideas in detail. All these ideas share two characteristics: first, they share a particular conception of what morality has to offer and second, they argue that what morality has to offer under this understanding is unsatisfactory; therefore, they call for changes in a variety of respects.

Anscombe sets the scene by presenting an account of morality as developed by consequentialist and deontological theories that owes much to a legislative or rule-governed model. She urges us to reject this account of ethics as it attempts to capture in precise, rigid rules, a topic whose very nature is complex, diverse and context specific. We should move away from a legalistic conception of morality, dominated by the notion of 'obligation', to a revival of the Aristotelian concepts of 'character' and 'virtue' as well as a renewed emphasis on the importance of moral psychology. Instead of asking 'What should I do here, now, with this specific problem?' we should be asking 'How should I live my life? What kind of person should I be?'

Bernard Williams starts from a similar point, a dissatisfaction with the notion of 'obligation' and the determining role it plays in deontological and consequentialist theories. Obligations are action focused, cannot conflict, leave no room for moral regret, commit us to the 'obligation out-obligation in' principle and apply to everyone without exception in such a way that we are always subject to blame for not fulfilling our obligations. This conception of 'obligations' causes a variety of problems, from forcing us to conceive of all sorts of concepts solely as obligations, to being committed to the view that only an obligation can beat an obligation, to having to accept that every obligation comes from a more general obligation. Instead of this narrow and limiting conception of morality, Williams urges us to embrace a wider conception of ethics.

This wider conception of ethics allows us to make sense of a more meaningful life for human beings. A life within which we can make sense of special commitments towards those we love that are justified by and understood within the very context of the relationships. A life which is not overwhelmed by the limiting demands of morality but which allows room for wider experiences and a fuller conception of what it means to live a good life; and a life which brings our motives into harmony with our reasons, values and justifications and avoids both the perils of moral schizophrenia and the drudgery of moral sainthood.

Finally, we have examined the concept of 'character' which is now central in this wider conception of ethics. We rejected the Kantian aspiration to a pure morality, in favour of a more plausible picture of character development as a gradual and difficult process, which is subject to many external factors and influences. One's moral character is distinctive, incorporates one's important commitments and values in a way that reflects who we really are and, after a lengthy period of development, leads to stable, predictable and dependable dispositions that express themselves in actions. This account of character development recognizes and accepts the inherent fragility of goodness as subject to the vagaries of luck, but as we shall see in the next part, this is both a plausible and a welcome picture; because only what is fragile and difficult to achieve is truly valuable and worth striving for.

Given that this is a volume on virtue ethics, the astute readers may have been surprised to see so little mention of virtue so far; however, as we shall come to see that in the next section everything we have discussed so far will go towards informing our account of virtue. We have concentrated on a negative picture, a critique of what is lacking in other alternatives, a call for change, and all of these ideas will now form the foundation of a more positive discussion that is to follow; a discussion that directly accounts for the advantages of virtue ethics.

Before we move on though, a note of caution. So far we have presented all these ideas in accordance with how they were first put forward by their proponents. As we have seen, this required a particular interpretation of morality as attributed to consequentialist and deontological theories; however, this interpretation could well be disputed. It may or may not have been the correct interpretation of what such theories had to offer at the time these discussions took place, but either way, what is certain is that both deontologists and consequentialists have responded to this type of critique by redefining, clarifying or refining their claims. For example, many deontologists have occupied themselves with showing how a modern Kantian can make room for an appropriate conception of the importance of friendship without falling foul of the kinds of objections raised in this section. Unfortunately, it is beyond the scope of this volume to explore these developments in full, but it is important to point out that the debate is not static and there are further responses to the line of attack outlined in this chapter and further rebuttals from virtue ethicists. In Chapter 9 of this volume, we will briefly consider how modern Kantians have responded to some of the concerns raised by virtue ethics, but before we do that we need to gain a better understanding of the positive claims made by virtue ethicists. So far, we have concentrated on a critical approach, one that found fault with other alternatives and one which explained virtue ethics in terms of what is it *not*, in terms of what it stands in opposition to. Now it is time to consider a more substantial account of virtue ethics as a viable alternative, as a theory that elaborates on positive claims beyond what other alternatives are available. In Part II, we will explore such an account of virtue ethics, broadly based under the idea of eudaimonistic virtue ethics.

PART TWO

Virtue ethics comes of age

CHAPTER FOUR

Virtue; an Aristotelian definition I

1. The primacy of virtue

In Part I, we discussed the sense of dissatisfaction with the two alternative normative theories, deontology and consequentialism, which led to calls for a revival of interest in virtue ethics. We looked at a number of different approaches which shared two characteristics, they all conceived of deontological and consequentialist claims in broadly the same, problematic manner, and they all called for radical revisions in the way we do moral theory, refocusing our attention on the notions of 'character' and 'virtue'. So far, the discussion has been quite critical and negative focusing on the shortcomings of others; however, the next stage in the development of virtue ethics is a much more positive project. Following these early calls for change, philosophers came forward willing to articulate what an alternative account of virtue ethics might look like. This is a much more constructive and positive project, as it focuses on building up a theory of virtue ethics and demonstrating its advantages almost regardless of what other alternatives have to offer. This part of the debate is more about the content and substance of virtue ethics rather than a critique of other normative theories.

One of the consequences of this shift of emphasis is that virtue ethics now becomes more of an umbrella term, subsuming a number of different and varied theories under the broader term. While the majority of these theories take their inspiration from Aristotelian ideas, this is by no means true of all of them. Some authors have been inspired to develop modern versions of virtue ethics based on the work of Plato, Hume and Nietzsche, works which now offer a variety of alternative interpretations of what it might mean to subscribe to virtue ethics. At the same time, some consequentialists and deontologists have responded to the challenges laid out by virtue ethics by showing how their theories are perfectly capable of incorporating the lessons of virtue without giving up on the main, distinctive claims of their own approach. At least some consequentialists and deontologists then have argued that their theories are perfectly capable of accounting for the insights of virtue ethics, which generates a distinction between *virtue ethics* and *theories of virtue*. In brief, theories of virtue are theories from all sorts of theoretical backgrounds that have some account of, or allow some room for, the concept of 'virtue'. Thus, a consequentialist could have something to say about the role of virtue in consequentialism, without thereby committing himself to virtue ethics. This is because virtue ethics is a normative account that places virtue at the centre of our understanding of what it is to live a good life. In some way or another, in virtue ethics, the concept of 'virtue' will be primary, central or of unique explanatory importance, something which is not true of *theories* of virtue.

In this part of the book, we will examine a particular account of virtue ethics, one which has probably been the most influential in discussions so far, eudaimonistic virtue ethics. In doing so, we will consider how virtue ethics has come of age in the sense of providing a substantial and detailed normative theory in its own right rather than merely a critique of other alternatives. In doing so, we will also make some sense of how the concept of 'virtue' is primary or central in virtue ethics in contrast to theories of virtue which merely make room for some account of virtue. We will look at the concept of 'virtue' in detail, something which we have not done so far, although, as we shall see, many of the ideas examined in Part I will play a pivotal role in constructing the account of virtue. Although we will mainly focus on eudaimonistic virtue ethics, we will touch upon some other alternatives. Finally, in Chapter 9, we shall have an opportunity to consider how other normative theories, namely deontology, can make room for the concept of 'virtue' without making it central to their understanding.

The idea that the concept of virtue has, somehow, a primary role to play in virtue ethics distinguishes virtue ethics from theories of virtue which may assign some importance to the virtues but not this primary role. For example, Julia Driver's consequentialist account allows room for the virtues, but under this account traits are virtues because they 'are valued by others as traits that morally improve the character possessing them . . . What makes these traits moral virtues is their tendency to produce beneficial effects'.[1] Thus, the judgement about the rightness of character, that is, virtue, is dependent on a judgement about the rightness or wrongness of actions. If a character trait produces good consequences, then it is a virtue and the main job of the theory is to give an account of what counts as good consequences. Driver, for example, goes on to elaborate that the virtues are traits that 'are valued because of their usefulness in easing social interaction'.[2] Similarly, a deontologist can find room for the concept of 'virtue' in his theory without relying on it to justify right conduct, so for the deontologist virtue is a disposition to do what is right, whereas for the virtue ethicist what is right is defined in terms of virtue. How this works out is developed in different ways by different virtue ethicists.

Gary Watson argues that virtue is theoretically dominant in virtue ethics because 'how it is best or right or proper to conduct oneself is explained in terms of how it is best for a human being to be'.[3] When we praise or blame someone for what they did, their behaviour, we are essentially praising or blaming them for who they *are*, their character. Right or wrong actions are mere manifestations of one's character and not grounds on which one's moral worth is justified upon. A second significant element of this primacy claim as presented by Watson is that the virtues are linked to who we essentially are as *human beings*, to what is characteristic of human lives, to what is in accordance with human nature. Not only that, but being virtuous is not merely instrumentally good but constitutive of what it means to live a good life *qua* human being. As we shall see below, both these claims are of central importance to eudaimonistic virtue ethics, but we will return to these points in more detail in Chapter 4, Section C. First we need to clarify a bit further what we mean when we say that praising someone for what they did involves praising them for who they are.

2. Doing the right thing is not enough

Generally, when we do the right thing, we should get credit for it, that is, we and other people should recognize that we behaved in morally admirable ways and we should get the praise we deserve. However, sometimes doing the right thing is not quite enough for moral praise. Consider the following cases where something good was done, but we are left with a sense of dissatisfaction, a concern that the person doesn't quite deserve moral praise. If we can articulate what is missing in these cases, perhaps, we can gain a better understanding of what is involved in being moral.

1   Kate has just discovered the internet. She has never been very confident with computers, but she has been encouraged to try to learn by her friends who assure her that she can get loads of bargains on line. In her first attempt to buy clothes online, she gets a bit flustered as loads of different windows keep popping up. Finally, she succeeds in spending £50 on a lovely new dress for herself. However, unknown to her, she has actually messed this up quite badly. In fact she has just donated £50 to a cancer research charity.

2   John is on his first date with Anne, whom he has admired from afar for quite a while. He has finally plucked up the courage to ask her out and is keen to make a good impression. They have gone on for a walk at the local park which is quite busy today as a news crew is filming a report on local wildlife. As John and Anne turn a quiet corner by the lake, they come across a young boy whose canoe has just capsized. The boy is in trouble and is shouting for help in between swallowing large amounts of water. John considers this an excellent opportunity to impress Anne and possibly get on the local news if he is lucky, so he has no hesitation in jumping in to heroically save the boy.

3   On Monday, Mary notices a homeless person sitting outside her office. She is having a slow day at the office so she walks out, approaches him, invites him to join her for lunch, gives him money for an overnight stay in a hotel and spends

two hours chatting to him about his life and how she can
help him. On Tuesday, she is in a hurry so she ignores him.
On Wednesday, she has loads of change weighing down her
purse so she tosses some money in his collection tin. On
Thursday, she is getting a bit fed up with the dirty, homeless
man in front of her and shouts at him to 'get a job!' On
Friday, she learns she has just gotten a big account, she's in
a great mood, so she invites him to celebrate with her at her
favourite restaurant.

The behaviour of all these people is problematic, not because of
what they did, because in general they managed to do good things,
for example, give to charity, save lives, help someone in need, but
rather because of *who they are* which colours what they did. Kate
has certainly done a good thing and the cancer research charity is
bound to put her money to good use, but it seems inappropriate to
praise her for doing something accidentally, by mistake, without
even being aware of what she has done. John has also produced a
good result in saving the boy but seems to have done it for the wrong
reasons. Wanting to impress one's girlfriend and seeking fame are not
the right reasons for saving someone's life. John should have saved
the boy's life *because* it needed saving and from a full appreciation
of the value of life, something that he would have done regardless
of whether the impressionable girlfriend and filming media were
there on that occasion. Mary's behaviour is erratic at best. On some
days she seems to behave kindly, but on others she, fairly arbitrarily
and for self-centred reasons, reverses her behaviour. This leads us
to question whether she really *ever* behaved kindly, because helping
others should be prompted by seeing the need in others and being
moved to assist them, not by arbitrary reasons such as whether
Mary herself is having a good day or not. It should be the homeless
person's ongoing need that consistently prompts Mary to respond,
rather than whatever else happens to be taking place in her life.

From all this, we can conclude that behaving morally involves
more than doing particular things, but rather doing them in a
particular manner. Aristotle counsels us:

> . . . virtuous acts are not done in a just or temperate way merely
> because *they* have a certain quality, but only if the agent also acts

in a certain state, viz. (i) if he knows what he is doing, (ii) if he chooses it, and chooses it for its own sake, and (iii) if he does it from a fixed and permanent disposition.[4]

Virtuous acts are not just acts that bring about certain consequences, but acts that proceed from particular states of character, virtuous states of character. Kate did not know what she was doing, she acted by mistake, John did not choose what he was doing for its own sake, he chose it as a means to impress others and Mary did not act from a fixed and permanent disposition, rather she acted in a fickle and unreliable manner. Neither of these three qualifies for virtue because of who they are which makes a difference to the quality of what they did.

Virtue ethics differs from both the consequentialist preoccupation with the importance of consequences and the deontological emphasis on the agent's motives. As we saw in the previous section, states of character are states of being expressed in doing, so, for example, the virtue of kindness will involve both a fixed and permanent disposition to respond in kind ways to situations that require a kind response and will result in kind actions. Importantly though, kind results are valued because they are part of virtue, rather than because of a claim that good and bad outcomes are intrinsically good and bad, respectively. The primacy of virtue, as discussed above, is preserved. When one merely produces good results by accident or from vicious motives, or from fickle and uncontrolled emotional responses, then one's actions despite the good results are not worthy of praise as they do not proceed from virtuous dispositions.

3. The function of human beings

In the sections that follow, we will, finally, be able to put together the elements of a definition of virtue. In order to do so, we need to look back over the ideas of Aristotle which have been central in these discussions. The reason we have taken such a circuitous route to get here, rather than starting with the Aristotelian definition, is that we will understand these Aristotelian ideas in a particular way, an interpretation which has been coloured and influenced by everything that has gone so far. The ideas we will be considering from now on are very firmly rooted in the Aristotelian tradition, but are not limited to a strict textual interpretation of Aristotle's works. Rather, they take inspiration from some Aristotelian ideas, interpret some other Aristotelian claims, enhance yet another set of Aristotelian theories and overall take the debate forward to create a comprehensive and independently viable conception of the virtues.

We saw above that Gary Watson's claim about the primacy of virtue contained two elements. The first is the idea that actions are mere manifestations of one's character and not grounds on which one's moral worth is justified upon, which we considered above. Now we will move on to consider the second element, namely that the virtues are linked to who we essentially are as human beings, to what is characteristic of human lives, to what is in accordance with human nature. Not only that, but being virtuous is not merely instrumentally good but constitutive of what it means to live a good life *qua* human being.

Aristotle's very first sentence in the *Nicomachean Ethics* is that '[e]very art and every investigation, and similarly every action and pursuit, aims at some good'.[5] Some of these activities have ends which we want for the sake of further ends, but there must be an end for which all else is done and which we value for its own sake. In order to lead meaningful lives, we need to discover this good for the sake of which we do everything else. Aristotle names this final good as eudaimonia. This is a term which is difficult to fully capture in translation. It is sometimes translated as 'happiness', but this is rather inadequate as happiness can be a transient feeling, dependent of external circumstances, which is easily upset and can apply to some aspects of one's life but not to others. Eudaimonia, on the other hand, is a persistent feeling of contentment or of fulfilment with one's life; it captures the idea of a flourishing life, a life well lived. Eudaimonia is not dependent on external factors, it cannot be easily upset and it refers to the entirety of one's life. What constitutes, then, the good life, the flourishing life, this life of eudaimonia?

Aristotle rejects the life of pleasure as the eudaimon life because pleasure is transient and can be put to both good and bad uses. For example, someone can derive pleasure from torturing kittens, but this doesn't make the torture of kittens right. Pleasure cannot be the object of the good life because the value of pleasure is determined by the value of the activity which gives rise to it and when the activity is evil, the pleasure derived from it is also evil. Similarly, he rejects the pursuit of honour, for honour depends on those who confer it. For example, corrupt regimes may confer honour on those who support them, but this 'honour' does not reflect the real moral value of the person's acts, rather it reflects what others think of him. Finally, he rejects the pursuit of wealth, as wealth is a means to other things and not a good in itself. The good life, the life we should be aiming at, must be a life which is truly characteristic of the person and can't be dependent on goods that are conferred by others, or goods that can be taken away or a life which reflects what others happen to think of one.

To find out what the eudaimon life consists in, perhaps, we should try a different approach; we should consider what is the good for human beings *qua* human beings. In the same way that in health, for example, the object of the activity, that for which all else is undertaken, is to restore health, and in military planning, the object of the activity is victory, there must be an object to living human lives. To discover this object, we must consider the function of human beings.

Aristotle observes that where a thing has a function the good of the thing, that is, when we say that the thing is doing well is when it performs its function well. The function of a knife is to cut; a good knife will be a knife that cuts well. The function of the eye is to see; a good eye will be one that has 20:20 vision. This argument will be applied to man; man has a function and the good man is the man who performs his function well. If we find out what the function of man is, we will know what the good life is, that is, it is the life that performs that function well.

To find the function of man, Aristotle asks us to look at what is distinctive of man. What is peculiar to man that sets him apart from other beings? For instance, humans take nourishment and they grow, but they share this with plants and animals, so eating and growing cannot be the distinctive function of human beings. Sentience is characteristic of human beings, but it is also shared by many animals so it can't be our distinctive function. The thing that humans alone possess, which we do not share with plants or animals, is reason. If the function of humans is reason, then the good human is the human who functions well, that is, reasons well, and this is the life of excellence. For Aristotle, the virtues are activities in accordance with reason, therefore they constitute the life of eudaimonia and that is why he devotes the rest of the book to considering what is involved in being virtuous. So eudaimonia, the good life for human beings, consists in reasoning well which is tantamount to being moral, being virtuous.

The type of argument developed above is called a teleological argument, from the Greek 'telos' for 'end' or 'purpose'. We will return to this kind of argument, objections against it and responses by virtue ethicists in Chapter 6, but for now we need to say a bit more about the definition of virtue.

4. The definition of virtue

When we think of virtue nowadays, we may think that the term is a bit old-fashioned or associated with specific Christian ideals of chastity, humility, self-sacrifice, etc. or perhaps that it is associated with a certain conservative view of morality. For Aristotle, however, virtue is moral goodness, moral excellence. Aristotle's definition of virtue is presented in Book II of the *Nicomachean Ethics*: 'Virtue is a purposive disposition, lying in a mean that is relative to us and determined by a rational principle, and by that which the prudent man would use to determine it'.[6] We will consider the elements of this definition one at a time.

For Aristotle, virtue is neither contrary to nor determined by our nature, rather we are shaped by nature to receive the virtues, provided we are exposed to the right kind of influencing and shaping factors. As we saw previously, when we discussed the concept of 'character', virtues as dispositional character traits will be shaped and developed over a long period of time and will be subject to the influence of numerous factors; however, once established, dispositions are stable, reliable, predictable and unshaken by temptations and distractions. The 'purposive' element of the definition refers to the fact that virtue is chosen, chosen knowingly and chosen for its own sake, for as we have seen above virtue cannot be accidental, mistaken or unintended. The Doctrine of the Mean further elaborates on these ideas.

Consider the following three scenarios and for each one ask whether the person's reaction/behaviour is appropriate, if yes, why so and if not, why not:

1 A group of friends are having a picnic on a nice sunny day. The food attracts a couple of wasps. Anne-Marie quickly gets up, upsets the picnic basket and runs away in fear.

2 Peter is a keen gardener. The front of his house is laid to
   lawn which is his pride and joy. He spends all his spare time
   ensuring that it is perfectly level, weed free and mowed to
   perfection. On a Sunday morning, Peter is looking out of his
   front window admiring his lawn only to see two local boys
   running all over it (the garden is unfenced). Peter rushes
   out, indignant and shouts at the boys. His chest swells with
   righteous anger and he lets it all vent in the direction of the
   boys who have polluted his lawn. The youngest of the boys
   bursts into tears and the eldest grabs him by the hand and
   runs off pursued down the road by Peter's screams, swears
   and threats.

3 Ernie, Tom and George are all foot soldiers during the
   World War I. Their regiment has just lined up and after
   a night of anxious waiting they are about to charge into
   enemy lines. The battle begins and Ernie rushes ahead
   of everyone else. He runs right towards the enemy lines
   without cover or protection. Tom finds his courage failing
   him and at the first opportunity he abandons his position
   and heads back towards the trenches. George stays with his
   comrades; he obeys orders to advance and retreat, remains
   in formation and does his best to play his role in the
   regiment.

Was Anne-Marie's reaction to the wasp appropriate? Hopefully, you
should have found it difficult give an answer to this question without
further information. If Anne-Marie has a severe allergic reaction
to wasp stings and has forgotten her emergency medication, then
running away in fear seems a fairly reasonable response. If, however,
she just doesn't like wasps, running away and ruining everyone's day
seems like an exaggerated response. Judging the appropriateness of
the response then cannot be done in isolation from knowing the
individual circumstances of the person. This is not the only relevant
point. Should it turn out that this was no ordinary wasp, but rather
a mutant, alien, 20-foot-tall wasp, then the question is no longer
why Anne-Marie ran away but why the rest of her friends didn't
follow closely at her heels. Running away in such circumstances is
no longer peculiar, but it's mandated by self-preservation; this time

it's the staying to face the 20-foot, mutant, alien wasp unperturbed while eating at the picnic that requires explanation. We can't judge the appropriateness of the reaction without knowing the individual circumstances of the person, the nature of the threat, the relationship between the two, etc. because all of these factors determine what will be an appropriate response. All of these factors will differ from one situation to the next and appreciating them will require a degree of good judgement. That means that the concept of 'appropriateness' does not operate in a vacuum, it's relative to the person and the circumstances and will change as these change.

Peter's reaction, however, seems rather exaggerated. Here, we have some more information about the situation and it seems that Peter's response to a relatively minor and harmless offence is exaggerated and causes quite a bit of unhappiness. The relevant point though is that although in this instance a display of a significant amount of anger is inappropriate and unwarranted by the details of the situation, this needn't always be the case. Had Peter been exposed to persistent bullying, including racial insults and the thread of physical harm, a significant amount of anger would have been the appropriate response. An excessive amount of feeling is not inappropriate in and of itself, nor can it be judged to be inappropriate in isolation of the circumstances that provoke it. Whether the feeling is appropriate or not will depend on what it is a reaction to and sometimes a strong response is the right one. This is exactly the idea captured by the concept of 'righteous indignation'. We would expect someone who was righteously indignant to be quite indignant, not merely a little bit upset. This amount of indignation is warranted though as it is proportional to the provocation. It is 'righteous' as the agent has a right to being this much indignant because of the gravity of the provocation. Indeed showing less than the right amount of righteous indignation, for example, remaining passive in the face of great insults, would lead us to question the agent's behaviour as perhaps lacking in appropriate self-respect. Sometimes the right thing is to be very angry and any other response just isn't good enough; however, a lot of anger is by no means the right response to every situation.

Finally, we have Ernie, Tom and George, three soldiers who behave in three completely different ways. Tom is clearly cowardly as he abandons his post and his comrades, but Ernie's behaviour also seems problematic. Where Tom suffers from an excess of fear, Ernie seems to suffer from an, equally problematic, lack of fear. Rushing into battle, heedless of any other considerations and with no regard for orders or what others are doing, may be as problematic in its rashness as cowardice is in the opposite direction. George seems to have the 'right amount' of fear, neither too much so as to turn him into a coward nor too little so as to make him rash. For courage is not the total absence of fear, that would be rashness, but the right amount of fear, which is appropriate to the nature of the situation. Faced with the enemy ranks in open battle should generate a good amount of fear and the virtue of courage cannot require one to be fearless regardless of the fear-provoking circumstances one is faced with. That wouldn't be courage but rashness or complete insensitivity to one's surroundings. Furthermore, we cannot prescribe, in advance of knowing the circumstances, what the courageous action might be. If the battle is going well, holding one's ground or advancing may be what is dictated by courage, but if the enemy threatens to overwhelm your position, a tactical retreat could be compatible with courage. Again, what is required is judgement to decide what is appropriate to the situation and the virtuous action cannot be captured in one prescriptive rule.

The above three examples capture some of the significant elements of the Doctrine of the Mean. The Doctrine of the Mean is essentially a claim about the importance and nature of the appropriate response. If we ask what is the right thing to do, then the answer cannot be general, but must be related to the particulars of the situation and the agent. Virtue is concerned with feelings and actions and in these respects one can go wrong erring either by excess or by deficiency. Fear is the feeling associated with the virtue of courage, but an excess of fear leads to the vice of cowardice, while a deficiency of fear leads to the vice of rashness. The correct amount of fear, the mean, is courage. However, the correct amount of the feeling, the mean, is not a mathematical mean. It's not an average of all possibilities, or a mathematical average, rather it is what is appropriate to the situation; very little fear is the appropriate response to a wasp by a person who does not suffer from any wasp allergies. Nor is it a doctrine of moderation, one that counsels a lukewarm emotional response to every situation; quite a lot of anger is the mean response to a serious insult. It is also a claim about the ways in which we can go wrong and fail to hit the mark of virtue, going wrong both by excess and by deficiency of feeling.

It will not be easy to find the mean in each situation for '. . . to feel or act towards the right person to the right extent at the right time for the right reason in the right way – that is not easy, and it is not everyone that can do it'.[7] Aristotle gives us some general advice for finding the mean response in different situations. We must keep away from the vice that is more contrary to the virtue. That is, some vices will appear more contrary to some virtues, for example, we have a natural inclination towards pleasures and this makes licentiousness (the excess of pleasures) seem more contrary to temperance (the virtue with respect to pleasures) than insensibility (the deficiency with respect to pleasures).[8] Also, we must be on our guard against pleasures as we are easily swayed by them, and we must be aware of and guard against our own particular weaknesses.[9] However, we must always remember that while there is only one appropriate response, that which reflects the particulars of the situation, there are many ways to go wrong and we can err by both excess and deficiency. Identifying and correcting our mistakes is not an easy process, getting it right involves both moral perception and practical wisdom, but everyone has the potential to go wrong in many different ways.

To summarize, the Doctrine of the Mean makes a number of complex and sometimes interrelated points:

1   feelings are part of choices and actions, and such feelings can be displayed in an excessive, deficient or 'just right' amount,

2   the 'just right' amount of feeling is not necessarily a moderate amount or a mathematical mean, but could be quite a lot depending on the circumstances of the case and the individual making the choice,

3   the right choice and action cannot be known in advance of the particulars of the case, so the mean is context sensitive and relative to the agent,

4   most importantly, that the Doctrine of the Mean is a doctrine of appropriateness, one which claims that what is appropriate in each situation will vary and it will be a matter of moral perception and moral judgement to decide the appropriate response in each situation and

5 finally that there are many ways to go wrong, but only
   one correct response in each situation, but that the one
   correct response is difficult to perceive and we may often
   be deceived by our own weaknesses and tendencies to go
   wrong.

Further readings

The Aristotelian ideas presented in this chapter are discussed in
Books I and II of the *Nicomachean Ethics*.

Gary Watson's influential paper on the primacy of virtue can be
found in, among other collections, Watson, in Statman, 1997. A
similar point about the primacy of aretaic concepts, like virtue, over
deontic concepts, like duty, is made by Slote in Baron et al., 1997.

For a more detailed analysis of Aristotle's function argument,
see Lawrence in Kraut, 2006, and linking the function argument to
other parts of Aristotelian theory, see McDowell, in Rorty, 1980.

Urmson's 'Aristotle's Doctrine of the Mean' available in Urmson,
in Rorty, 1980, is an excellent analysis of the concept, while
Hursthouse's paper in Kraut, 2006, offers an alternative, compelling
analysis of the doctrine.

CHAPTER FIVE

Virtue; an Aristotelian definition II

1. The role of the ideally virtuous agent

One of the original concerns with deontology and consequentialism was that the reliance of these theories on rules meant that they could not give an accurate account of ethics, so it is only fair that we ask how virtue ethics resolves this problem. If deontology and consequentialism rely on rigid rules that do not represent the nature of the subject matter, at least they have the advantage of giving us concrete guidance. By rejecting these rules, virtue ethics risks failing to offer *any* action guidance whatsoever, and surely we would expect a moral theory to give us some specific help with what we should do when faced with moral problems. Our inquiries into morality have a practical purpose; they are about the way we act so it is reasonable to expect moral theories to offer some guidance in this respect. Rules may be rigid and inflexible but at least they offer concrete guidance; if virtue ethics rejects rules, what does it replace them with and does it succeed in offering any action guidance?

One possible response on the part of the virtue ethicist is to point to the role of the virtuous agent in the theory. After all, the very definition of virtue appeals to the notion of the virtuous agent, so if we want action guidance we should appeal to the ideally virtuous agent, the one who has all the answers, and follow his example.

Virtue ethics would then be action guiding because it guides us to do as the virtuous agent does. However, there are a number of immediate problems with this suggestion:

1   First we face a practical problem: what *would* the ideally virtuous agent do? If we have problems identifying what we, the less than ideally virtuous agents, the ones who are confused, tempted, side-tracked and perplexed by morality, should do, how can we know what the ideally virtuous agent would do?

2   We may appeal to an actual virtuous agent and follow his example which would at least reveal what he does when faced with moral problems, but how do we identify the virtuous agent in the first place? Moral questions seem to be rife with conflicting answers and lively debate, how do we identify within this plurality of views which account of the right answer corresponds to the ideally virtuous agent?

3   Since our main focus is the agent's character, which is habitually but not necessarily exemplified in his actions, we will have a further epistemological difficulty of correctly establishing the person's moral character. Even if we managed to identify someone who habitually did the right thing, we wouldn't know if he did it for the right reasons and was truly virtuous.

4   Even if we could identify the virtuous agent, it is not clear that observing him could help us. Since his choices do not rely on a rule or principle, there is no easy rule or principle he could reveal to us to give us guidance. What he does may appear conflicted to us as external observers, and the reasons behind his actions may remain entirely opaque. How can the ideally virtuous agent go about helping us follow his example even if he is inclined to help us?

5   Even if he finds a way of accounting for his actions, why should we think that what is right for him is also right for us? Given everything we have said about the context sensitivity of ethics, how the Doctrine of the Mean suggests

the answer will be relative to the person and to the situation and so on, it seems contradictory to now expect to be able to follow another person's example to the letter. Not only would the student need to come across an identical situation to the ideally virtuous agent but also, since the agent is part of determining the correct response, the student himself would need to be identical to the ideally virtuous agent in order for one and the same choice and action to be appropriate for both. Even as ideal, it is not clear how an ideally virtuous, perfect agent could help non-ideal, imperfect agents like us.

6 Indeed aspiring to an ideal which we fail to achieve may turn out to be detrimental to us. Attempting to become what is beyond our ability may lead to harmful distortions. To take an example of Nietzsche's, altruism without the inner strength required for the virtue proper, may turn into a distorted, self-centred, helping of others by way of self-promotion which is clearly not virtue.

The action guidance objection does not only have purely practical aspects but also affects the conceptual understanding of virtue ethics. Creating a link between the account of right action and the ideally virtuous agent, such that right action is defined in terms of what the ideally virtuous agent would do, leaves us wondering what is it exactly that he would do and would it be possible for non-ideally virtuous agents to figure this out? Furthermore, we are left to wonder whether the ideally virtuous agent can ever get it wrong or whether it is even possible for two ideally virtuous agents to disagree about the right course of action.

One possible response to this problem is to acknowledge that it is a problem, but it's no more or less a problem for virtue ethics than it is for consequentialist or deontological theories. A consequentialist theory might, for example, link right action to good consequences, but the question still remains what counts as a 'good consequence', how do we differentiate between different kinds of good consequences, how do we weigh up the competing claims of different consequences, etc. Similarly, a deontological theory might, for example, link right action to the test of the

Categorical Imperative, but the question still remains: how do we formulate the maxim to be tested by the Categorical Imperative? Is the maxim in question 'Never lie' or 'Protect innocent lives'? The same qualities of judgement and wisdom which are required in determining what count as good consequences may be at play in deciding how to formulate the maxim to be tested or how to determine what the ideally virtuous agent would do in our place. Virtue ethics owes us further answers, but they are not peculiar to the theory, they are the same type of answers owed to us by the other kinds of theories as well.

In what follows, I will try to elaborate on one possible direction virtue ethics could take in providing more content for these answers, but I will suggest that the role of the ideally virtuous agent has been misrepresented both in the objections above and in the virtue ethical answers to them that rely to an excessive extent on the role of the virtuous agent.

2. The *orthos logos*

If virtue ethics itself makes the mistake of relying to an excessive extent on the role of the virtuous agent, it is not the fault of its detractors that they point out the many possible difficulties with the application of the concept. The solution is, perhaps, to reinterpret the role of the ideally virtuous agent in the first place. To do this, we need to return to the Aristotelian definition of virtue: 'Virtue is a purposive disposition, lying in a mean that is relative to us and determined by a rational principle, and by that which the prudent man [the ideally virtuous agent] would use to determine it'.[1] It is the presence of the ideally virtuous agent in the definition that might prompt us to give him such a prominent role in understanding the theory, but that would be a misreading of the definition. Virtue is determined by a rational principle and by what the ideally virtuous man would use to determine *the rational principle*, so perhaps our focus should be on the rational principle rather than the ideally virtuous agent.

However, our readers may begin to feel a bit cheated now. We started off with the virtue ethical critique of the role of rules and principles in moral philosophy and the rejection of such an approach in favour of an alternative; the search for the alternative brought us to the ideally virtuous agent, but appeal to him seems to be deeply problematic, are we to just return to rules then? No, the problem here is one of translation. The original term usually translated as 'rational principle' or 'right principle' is *orthos logos* and the usual translations of the term are rather misleading. Aristotle gives us no examples of rules whatsoever in the *Nicomachean Ethics* which would be a bizarre choice if his final appeal was to rules or principles. A more correct translation for *orthos logos* is 'according to a correct appreciation of the situation'.[2] Thus, the *orthos logos* is both particular, it has to do with the situation specific details of the circumstances one finds oneself in and it was to do with an *appreciation* of these specifics, an ability to perceive, understand, judge and be motivated by these specifics. We will consider what is involved in perceiving, understanding, judging and being motived by specific features of situations in the next two sections, when we discuss moral perception and practical wisdom. These concepts will give us an insight into what it is that the ideally virtuous person does when he determines the *orthos logos* and will explain what we should aim to do, that is, see the ideally virtuous person as an exemplar of *how* to think not an exemplar of *what* to think.

3. Moral perception

The ideally virtuous agent is not merely someone who does the right thing. As we have seen, the right action is not necessarily a guarantee of virtue, what we need to look at is the person's character. Our appeal to the ideally virtuous person makes sense because it is an 'appeal made not just to what the virtuous person would do but to the kind of person that the virtuous person is'[3] and he is the kind of person who appreciates the *orthos logos*.

Indulge me for a moment. After reading the following description, close your eyes and imagine it: you come home from your lecture one afternoon and the moment you see your housemate and best friend you know that something is not right. She is not her usual bubbly self; she is uncommunicative and withdrawn. Knowing that she's had problems with her boyfriend you suspect things have taken a turn for the worst but you also know that she will talk to you about it when she is ready. You cancel your cinema plans for the evening and instead sit with her waiting for her to be ready to talk. Unfortunately, you were right, her boyfriend left her and she is very depressed about the whole thing. The two of you spend the evening chatting and finish off a huge tub of ice cream while singing 'I will survive' at the top of your lungs. Before going to bed she gives you a huge hug and you know that although things are not fine yet, she is feeling better and you have helped.

Now you might immediately reply that your best friend would never be a wreck because of a break-up or that if she was she wouldn't keep quiet about it or that she hates ice cream anyway, or a million other objections to the particulars of the situation, but in that case you should change the details to suit your experience with your particular best friend. Put in whatever it is that your friend cares about and whose loss would upset her, give her the correct reaction to grief, imagine the details you would notice that would alert you to that particular person's change in emotional outlook, fill in the details as to what you would do to make her feel better given the kind of person she is and the kind of friendship you have and so on. The actual details are not important as such for our purposes, more the ability to imagine the scenario, immerse yourself in it and consider what it is that you do when you come across such situations, because you do quite a lot of things.

First, you observe changes and differences, changes which you can only observe in virtue of knowing the person so well in the first place. These observations need not be conscious, nor do you need to be able to list them, they may be subtle signs that you take on board without necessarily having them at the forefront of your conscious awareness. Second, you bring together rational and emotional capacities to bear on the situation. You remember her previous boyfriend troubles, you imagine what it must be like for her to be in this situation, you empathize with affairs of the heart gone wrong, you consider what you could do to help, etc. Third, you form a plan of action in direct relation to what you have perceived, for example, you cancel your cinema plans because she is unhappy and because you judge she may need company. Again not everything you do has to be consciously thought out, when you give her a hug, this is a spontaneous reaction to her eyes tearing up and you don't need to have consciously preplanned all your reactions. However, what is important is that your behaviour is governed by the specifics of her situation, by seeing her upset, by seeing her tearful, by imagining her pain, etc., and by your understanding of friendship and kindness, for example, the idea that friends support each other, that kindness requires that we do not abandon those in need. What you are doing is exercising Aristotelian perception and Aristotelian practical wisdom.

Wiggins writes:

> A man usually asks himself "What shall I do?" not with a view to maximizing anything but only in response to a particular context. This will make particular and contingent demands on his moral or practical perception, but the relevant features of the situation may not all jump to the eye. To see what they are, to prompt the imagination to play upon the question and let it activate in reflection and thought-experiment whatever concerns and passions it should activate, may require a high order of situational appreciation, or, as Aristotle would say, perception.[4]

We have seen how ethics is a context sensitive enterprise, and now we see how situational appreciation, or moral perception, is the ability to perceive context sensitivity. Faced with a complex, detailed and context-specific world, we have the ability to perceive moral features in a way analogous to how the eye perceives visual features. In the same way that visual features 'jump out' at us when we view a scene, moral features 'jump out' at us when we come across a moral situation. In the same way that some people have better vision or are more visually perceptive than others, some people have better moral perception or are more morally perceptive than others. When you walk into the room you perceive the change in your friend's conduct and this is not merely a matter of seeing what she is doing, but also feeling and imagining what has happened to her. It is because you know your friend so well in virtue of your friendship that you are able to perceive the changes and understand their importance.

Contrast this account of a morally active world with the Humean account of a morally inert world. According to Hume, if we examine an act, for example, murder, we cannot find anything in the act itself that accounts for its being a vice. Hume writes: 'The vice entirely escapes you as long as you consider the object. You can never find it, till you turn your reflection into your own breast, and find a sentiment of disapprobation, which arises in you, towards the action'.[5] The world of facts reveals nothing about the

morality of murder, to understand the moral tenor of the act you
need to look inside you, towards your own feelings and sentiments
of disapproval of the act. Hume sees the world as a matter of
morally inert facts and draws a sharp distinction between the role
of reason, to perceive these facts, and the role of feelings, to give
us insights into morality. The account of moral perception we have
developed so far denies both of these approaches. It views the world
as a source of moral value, one that is perceived, using both rational
and affective faculties, by the agent.

Some moral features of situations are easily perceived by almost
anyone. If you come across a lake with a drowning baby, the
drowning baby should become immediately obvious to you as a
morally significant feature of the situation, whereas the colour of the
sky, the swans in the distance and the oak trees changing colour, all
pale into moral insignificance given the fact of the drowning baby.
While the colour of the sky, the swans and the beautiful trees are
perfectly noteworthy in other contexts, for example, in a situation
where there is no drowning baby and you are merely looking for
a good spot for a watercolour painting, they fade into the moral
perceptual background given the presence of the drowning baby.
However, other moral features of situations may be more difficult
to perceive. If your friend is a very private person, who shows little
of her inner turmoil to the external world, it may take a very good
friend to perceive a subtle change in her conduct which betrays
her grief. And it is part of our understanding of friendship that
it will involve an intimate knowledge of the friend, a knowledge
which is not available to strangers and casual acquaintances, but a
knowledge which forms part of the trust and understanding which
is an essential ingredient of friendship. Not all particulars are easily
perceived by just about anyone, some are only noticeable from
privileged positions like that of a friend.

It is important to note here that although salient particulars will
change from one situation to another, so that for one friend it's ice-
cream and Aretha Franklin, whereas for another it's a pint of beer
and The Red Hot Chilly Peppers, this does not mean that there is
no one objectively correct answer. Ice-cream and Aretha Franklin
are the right answer for this friend, at this time, in this situation and
as offered by you and this is compatible with another answer being
right for a different friend, at a different time and in a different

situation. There is one correct answer for each situation, but that one answer is not correct for all situations.

When virtue ethics rejects the appeal to rules it replaces it with the ideally virtuous agent, not so much with what he does, but rather with the kind of person he is and he is the kind of person who has the ability to perceive morally salient particulars. When we look to the ideally virtuous person, we look to the ability to perceive morally salient particulars and this is something that we can educate ourselves in over time and something we can learn from others even if they themselves are not ideally virtuous. This is because the ability to perceive morally salient particulars is situation-specific and it is plausible to assume that some people will be better in some situations and contexts than others, so the trick is to seek guidance and role models in those situations and contexts in which others are successful. What we are looking for is examples of how to be, rather than precise descriptions of what to do, so we can learn from how others get it right (and wrong) rather than merely copying what they are doing.

Now you may wonder whether you have received any real help with action guidance here. One possible objection is that this ability to perceive morally salient features is rather mysterious and it is only supported by an argument by analogy, that is, the analogy with sight. However, when it comes to sensations and experiences, arguments by analogy can work rather well. Consider the following account of pain in terms of sound: 'My leg began to declare itself in a way that I can only describe in terms of sound; from a mute condition it began to murmur, then to moan and whine, then to scream'.[6] The author chooses to use sound to describe the pain to really engage the reader's senses and move him to almost feel the pain himself. This strategy works on activating the reader's imagination, putting him in the fictional character's shoes, making him live through the experience, and it achieves this a lot better than simply saying 'It hurt, it hurt a lot' ever would. By transferring the escalation of the sound to the idea that the pain increased, we get a more immediate and moving sense of what it felt to experience the pain. When philosophers claim that moral perception is like sight, they are inviting their readers to 'see' situations in this particular way. This is why claims about moral perception are often accompanied by detailed examples of moral situations, often borrowed from works of literature. A book affords the time and space to really develop the details of a case and authors have the skill to bring such details to life. The argument for moral perception is not merely an analogy but an invitation to immerse oneself into a particular way of thinking, to experience a situation in all its subtleties and share in a moral experience. The process of developing moral perception is a gradual one, subject to the right education and subject to exposing ourselves to the rights sorts of situations.

If at the end of all this, having immersed ourselves in particulars, we still find that moral disagreement is still very much present, we mustn't despair – after all Aristotle did warn us that the subject matter is complex and difficult, so perhaps we shouldn't be surprised that coming up with answers may be a life-long project.

4. Practical wisdom

If moral perception allows the virtuous man to see what is required of him, practical wisdom, or prudence, shows him *why* it is required of him. Virtue is a purposive disposition concerned with choice; choice involves both the right reasoning and the right desire, and practical wisdom is the ability to make virtuous choices.

> Now the origin of action (the efficient, not the final cause) is choice, and the origin of choice is appetition [desire] and purposive reasoning [reasoning directed to some end]. Hence choice necessarily involves not only intellect and thought, but a certain moral state; for good conduct and its contrary necessarily involve thought and character.[7]

Practical wisdom is not merely a theoretical capacity to reason about the noble and the good, but also a practical one to do what is noble and good because one both knows what is right and has a disposition to do what is right. It's a capacity to see what is required by the noble and the good in terms of choice and action; the ability to both deliberate well and to act on that deliberation. To understand practical wisdom, we need to understand Aristotelian choice and how it brings together reason and the emotions. In what follows, we will consider the ideal case of the virtuous agent whose reason and emotions are in perfect harmony and flow effortlessly into action. In Chapter 7, we will come back to this claim and consider what happens with those of us who are less than ideally virtuous and whose reason and desires are not in perfect harmony. However, before we consider how things can go wrong, we should understand the ideal case.

The question of the relation between reason and the emotions in general has a very rich philosophical history. Modern moral philosophy is greatly influenced by the Humean picture of reason and desire as being two separate elements of action. Reason provides information, for example, beer can be found at the pub, while desire provides motivation, for example, I want beer, which results in the action of going to the pub to drink beer. The influence of this Humean account is so great that even those who reject it still hold on to the idea that reason and desire are two separate elements of action. Interestingly enough, I think that Aristotle did not subscribe to this division. His account of reason and the emotions did not seem to start from the idea that they are separate, nor did he see only one element as (primarily) responsible for motivating action. To understand why that is, we need to consider how reason and desire operate in the virtuous person.

The virtuous person's emotions are not emotions he happens to have but stable, reliable emotions, purposefully cultivated to go along with and support the demands of reason. His character traits are cultivated emotional sensitivities that have been developed *because* of the sorts of dispositions that they are. He chooses to have particular emotions because they result in particular sensitivities, particular ways of seeing the world and particular ways of being motivated by it. And the way he sees the world is both emotional and rational, abilities that are intertwined and mutually dependent, rather than separate and at odds with each other. The process of gradual development from doing 'the that' to understanding 'the because' which we considered in Part I, is neither exclusively rational nor exclusively emotional. It's a process that involves coming to fully appreciate the noble and the good, understanding and internalizing not just what we must do, but *why* we must do it *because* it is the right thing to do; '[t]his is why chosen actions are the best indicators of character – because they embody, express, or reflect the agent's conception of the good'.[8] The notion of 'choice' ensures that a good action is not done merely coincidentally in accordance with the right reason, but rather that it embodies the right reason, that it is done because of the right reason: '. . . virtue is not merely a state in conformity with the right principle, but one that implies the right principle'.[9]

The virtuous person does not have a neutral conception of facts, to which he adds a separate desire in order to result in action; rather, our approach rejects the view of the world as motivationally inert. The virtuous person's conceptualization of the particular facts includes emotive and motivational aspects. The realization that 'she is in pain' includes an emotional response to that pain and motivation to do something to alleviate the pain. The habituation required for virtue involves exactly this ability to see particulars in situations in a special light, that is, as constituting reasons for action and means that one cannot share a virtuous person's way of seeing a situation without also sharing his reasons to act[10]; 'one's detailed grasp of what is involved in acting virtuously, in acting for the *right* reasons, is not separable from one's grasp of what each of the virtues involves, and one's grasp of that is not separable from possession of the virtues themselves'.[11]

Aristotle understands choice as 'rational desire' or 'emotional reason', without placing emphasis or priority on either reason or desire. And human beings are the union of reason and desire which results in action. We are judged by our choices, by how our reasoning and our desires come together to produce action, and the choices of the ideally virtuous man proceed from the rational wish (*boulesis*), which is a rational longing for the noble and the good. Practical wisdom then has a particular connection to virtue. Anyone can be clever in the sense of applying their intelligence to whatever ends they happen to want to achieve, but practical wisdom aims at the good. This means that although vicious people may exhibit what, to outsiders, may look like virtue, their behaviour is not really virtue as it doesn't aim at the good. Imagine a burglar who steals for personal gain because of greed and laziness, but he accomplishes his burglaries with a lot of courage. He does not shy from dangerous situations, he remains cool under pressure but shows a prudent and controlled amount of fear, etc., all of which looks a lot like the virtue of courage. If this were indeed the virtue of courage, we would have a problem here as we would have a vicious person displaying virtue in the pursuit of vicious ends. However, this isn't really the virtue of courage as it does not aim at the good. Many people can display appropriate reactions to fear, which look like the virtue of courage, but unless they are aimed at the right ends, these displays are mere mockeries of virtue. This false courage bears the same relation to the virtue of courage as a shadow bears to the woman who casts it; both are monochrome, flat renditions of the original. Practical wisdom is the ability which distinguishes what kinds of fears one should aim to face, so that facing one's fear in a pursuit of a just cause, the virtue of courage, is distinguished from facing one's fear in pursuit of personal gain and self-indulgent pleasure, false courage.

Since practical wisdom is a disposition to make correct emotional judgements in choices relating to the noble and the good, it underlies all the virtues and unites them in the sense that it gives us a unified view to our lives as a whole. If kindness is the disposition to respond kindly to situations which require kindness, one cannot be kind unless one has a correct conception of all sorts of other virtues like fairness, loyalty, trustworthiness, etc., all of which may also be relevant in different situations. Since all the virtues may be present in all sorts of combinations in different situations, being sensitive to virtue in one respect must also involve being sensitive to virtue in all other respects.

It is also important to note that practical wisdom does not provide a blueprint or application guide for specific situations that is then applied top down when one comes across a problem. Rather, practical wisdom contains a conception of the noble and the good which is to be found in the specifics of situations; practical wisdom gives one a conception of what it means to live a eudaimon life, but part of this is the propensity to put that end into practice as required by particular circumstances. And the way to practical wisdom is through habituation and action: 'Someone who has been properly brought up has been habituated into seeing the appropriate actions as worth going in for in the specific way that is expressed by bringing them under the concept of the noble'.[12] 'Going in for' in this quote means not just merely doing, but choosing, choosing knowingly and choosing for their own sake. So habituation, becoming just by performing just acts, imparts to the agent both a conceptual understanding of why the noble and the good should be chosen for their own sake and the emotional maturity to make these choices.

The result of habituation is a motivational tendency, but one with a conceptual and hence rational aspect. People with a properly formed character have learned to see certain actions as worth undertaking on the ground that they are noble; they have acquired that reason-giving concept, on a way that is inextricably bound up with acquiring the propensity to be motivated by thoughts in which it is applied.[13]

Having considered the Aristotelian definition of virtue, we should now return to the role of teleology in Aristotle's function argument, a question we suspended at the time in Chapter 4 Section C, but should consider in fuller detail now.

Further readings

There are numerous discussions of the role of the virtuous agent in virtue ethics. Russell, 2009, Chapter 4, section 1, has a good summary with references of the main commentators who discuss the role of virtuous agent. The critical concerns with the role of the virtuous agent discussed in this chapter are raised more in-depth by Louden, in Statman, 1997, while Solomon in the same volume considers and replies to objections about the role of the virtuous agent and action guidance in virtue ethics. Hursthouse's seminal paper, reprinted in Crisp and Slote, 1997, defends the argument that virtue ethics is no more and no less action guiding than other normative theories.

This chapter has been influenced in large part by a series of papers written either in response or inspired by each other. The first is David Wiggins's, reprinted in Rorty 1980, where he first develops the notion of 'situational appreciation' or 'moral perception' in Aristotelian thought. This paper is closely followed by John McDowell's 1978 paper written in reply to Philippa Foot's 1972 contribution. McDowell's very influential arguments in this area are further developed in McDowell, 1979, and McDowell, in Engstrom and Whiting, 1996a.

For further discussions, see Annas, 1993, Chapter 2 develops excellent accounts of the Aristotelian virtuous person (section 5) and practical wisdom (section 3), as well as Hursthouse, 1999 (Part 1 on the virtuous agent and action guidance and Part 2 on Aristotelian choice), while Korsgaard in Engstrom and Whiting, 1996 develops an Aristotelian account of choice and it's relation to the noble and the good.

CHAPTER SIX

A naturalistic account
of virtue

1. Teleology; a discredited account?

In Chapter 4, Section C above, we saw how Aristotle used the function argument to discover the good life (eudaimon life) for human beings. His answer was linked to what human beings are for *qua* human beings, their distinctive characteristic, which turned out to be the ability to reason. A life lived in accordance to the dictates of reason is the life of virtue, so at that point we pushed on with that discussion to better understand the concept of 'virtue'. Now we can return to the function argument and question what is involved in relying on a teleological account. In this section of the chapter, we will consider some of the objections and criticisms which led moral philosophers to be weary of teleological arguments, the next section will consider Aristotle's account of teleology and whether it is indeed vulnerable to these objections, while Section C will consider the Aristotelian answer to the problem of moral luck and Section D will look at how modern virtue ethicists, Rosalind Hursthouse and Philippa Foot, have developed versions of teleological arguments.

Just before we move on to examine the critiques of teleology, we should take one moment to consider in a bit more detail what is involved in making a teleological claim. Suppose we were to seek to understand the nature of 'chairs' in a teleological manner, we would need to ask 'what is characteristic of chairs?' Chairs can be made of many different materials, they can be made of wood, or plastic or leather, etc., they come in many different sizes, styles and shapes, some have arms, others do not, many have four legs but it is possible to have a chair with three legs and so on. So neither material, size or other physical descriptions seem to capture what is *essential* about the concept of a 'chair' but nonetheless a plastic, self-assembly, kitchen chair still has something essentially in common with a leather and wood, hand-worked, antique living room chair. A better way of capturing what is characteristic of chairs is to ask what chairs are for. The answer is that chairs are for sitting on. Other objects may also be used for sitting on, for example, sofas, and at the same time chairs may be used for other purposes, for example, for standing on to reach high up, but fundamentally the purpose of a chair is to provide a functional place to sit on. What all chairs have in common is that their purpose is to serve as somewhere to sit and we understand the concept of a good chair in relation to how well it serves this function. A chair with a really small, and therefore uncomfortable, seating area would not be a good specimen of the kind under this description. While this account may work for chairs though, it's not immediately clear that it works for human beings and nature in general.

One of the most important critiques of teleological arguments is that they are outdated and proven to be invalid by modern scientific advances. Teleological arguments focus on the existence of a *telos*, an end, a final cause towards which nature is aiming, the scientific revolution however has brought with it a better understanding of nature according to which nature is not purposeful in this relevant sense. We have understood the natural world around us by abandoning the assumption that animals and other elements of nature aim at a particular final cause. A giraffe does not have a long neck because it is aiming, as a species, to elongate its neck, rather it has a long neck because of evolutionary reasons, for example, creatures with longer necks were at an evolutionary advantage in an environment which offered food at the top branches of tall trees. Bertrand Russell points out how teleology was abandoned as science found mechanistic questions about the causes of things such as 'What caused giraffes to have long necks?' to yield much more useful answers in terms of scientific knowledge than teleological questions such as 'What final purpose does the giraffe's long neck serve?'[1] Russell sees the Aristotelian understanding of nature as conceptually tied to the scientifically outdated idea of teleology. He interprets Aristotelian nature as aiming at a certain conclusion and as belonging 'to the class of causes which operate for the sake of something'.[2] Evolutionary theory teaches us otherwise, nature does not have a purpose, what appears to be a matter of design is in fact a matter of change through inherited characteristics caused by environmental adaptation. Natural selection does not aim at a final purpose, rather it is an adaptive process in response to environmental factors and the notion of a 'teleological nature', nature with a purpose, an end, a final cause, is scientifically outdated.

One possible way out of these difficulties for teleology is to posit a creator. The teleological explanation of the function of chairs seems to work very well because there is a creator behind each chair who made it with its specific function, that is, to be sat upon, in mind. If we posit a creator behind the whole of nature, we can retain the idea of purpose, final cause or *telos* for the natural order. Nature has a purpose because it was created for a purpose by a being that could imbue it with this purpose. The problem with this solution though is that its acceptance is conditional on the acceptance of the idea of the existence of a creator. As philosophers, we expect our arguments to have universal appeal and we expect moral views to be convincing to a broad audience; however, this strategy, while solving the problem of the apparent lack of purpose in nature, only does so by positing a being that gave nature its purpose. As a result it is only satisfactory as a view to those who accept the existence of this being in the first place and will fail to convince those who doubt the existence of such a being.[3]

Another criticism of the Aristotelian account of teleology is that it is anthropocentric, that is, it places human beings in a privileged, central and controlling position in the natural world. Instead of conceiving humans as, perhaps equal but at the very least equally important, a part of the natural world, it conceives of them as the entity around which all others are organized. The natural world is there to serve our purposes, to aid us in fulfilling our ends, rather than having intrinsic value of its own. For example, David Sedley argues that for Aristotle since mother's milk exists for the sake of her babies, then all food exists for the sake of the humans who consume it, which makes the purpose of all animals we eat, to be our nourishment, that is, they exist for us to eat them.[4] This makes the existence and importance of the entire natural world conditional on serving our purposes.

A further concern with teleology accepts the general approach of the theory, but questions how we identify the purpose of an object or organism. For example, pigs can be eaten by humans or used to provide transplant organs for humans, so why not pick either of these two purposes as the final end of pigs rather than focusing on the pigs' individual survival and species continuation? Out of the three functions, continuation of the pig species, nutrition for humans or provision of organs for transplants for humans, which is the correct function for pigs and how can we pick one over the others?[5]

Finally, to what is already a long list of concerns, we should add a series of criticisms that relate to the naturalistic aspect of teleology. These kinds of objections might apply to all theories that appeal to nature to give an account of morality. The criticism is that what occurs in nature is a matter of description, it is just what happens, rather than a matter of morality, that is, a question of what should happen, and we must not confuse what *is* with what *should be*. A description of how things are in nature does not answer normative questions about how we should behave. Consider, for example, the following natural fact: human beings are carnivorous. This is clearly true, humans are both able to eat animal meat and derive nutrition from doing so, but it doesn't help with the normative question about whether we *should* eat animal meat. Arguments for vegetarianism do not deny that we are naturally able to eat meat; rather they argue that we morally should not do so. So knowing what we naturally do doesn't help with knowing what we should do.

Furthermore, naturalistic accounts of ethics make the mistake of thinking that what occurs in nature is by definition benign, welcome and something that we should not seek to alter by virtue of its being natural. Clearly, however, this can't be true. Nature includes a good dose of cruelty, suffering and pain, all of which cannot be morally acceptable simply because they occur naturally. Finally, what is natural is often confused with what is statistically predominant; 'normal' in a probabilistic sense of what is likely to occur, but surely statistics should not generate moral precepts. Just because something is what the majority happen to do, isn't a good enough argument for what we should do.[6] As my mother used to say to me frequently when I was young 'If everyone else jumped out of the window, would you follow suit?!'

2. Aristotle on teleology

Having looked at the kinds of objections that led to the dismissal of teleological arguments from much of modern moral philosophy, we will now consider possible replies on behalf of teleology. First, we will consider how these objections may be addressed from an Aristotelian viewpoint by looking at interpretations of Aristotle's own works which may give us replies to these concerns. Then, we will go on to consider how modern virtue ethicists, Rosalind Hursthouse and Philippa Foot, have redeveloped and progressed Aristotelian teleology. In between the two discussions, we will consider the Aristotelian response to the problem of moral luck, but more on this in the next section.

We will start our discussion in reverse order and consider first the arguments against naturalistic accounts of ethics. Suppose we seek an account of normativity independent of our nature in order to avoid the objections above, where would this account of normativity emerge from? We would have to give an account that had no connection to what we are like as a species, that is, that we are social animals, who care for their young, who are capable of empathy, etc. and such an account risks being entirely disconnected from the kind of beings that we are and the way we live our lives. While an exclusive reliance on how we are like naturally risks confusing descriptive facts with normative conclusions, a severe divorce between normativity and nature risks resulting in nonsensical conclusions that have no particular relevance for beings such as such. As a species that has normative concerns in the first place we are concerned with ethical questions exactly because of the kinds of beings that we are. While difficult to assert categorically, it does seem plausible that fish, for example, lack the specific ethical concerns of human beings, and therefore the good life for fish can be identified without reference to the ethical connections that both challenge and enrich the life of humans. To find out what the good life consists in for fish, we need to consider them as a species and the same goes for humans. To conceive of normativity as entirely separate and unaffected from what we are characteristically like as a species is to deprive us of an understanding of normativity *for people like us*.

This account does not make the mistake of identifying the natural with the normative, but rather paints a picture of the normative as deriving from the natural; therefore, what a species is naturally like will have an enormous impact on how we understand normativity for that species. Normativity is connected to our nature, and similarly we can draw on nature to understand what is involved in the good life for other species.

> What is helpful for ethics from this kind of biological naturalism is that we find that the normativity of our ethical discourse is not something which emerges mysteriously with humans and can only be projected back, in an anthropomorphic way, onto trees and their roots. Rather, we find normativity in the realm of living things, plants and animals already.[7]

The good life for humans will be determined in the same way that we determine the good life for fish or for pigs by asking what is the characteristic way of being for that species *qua* species. What is the characteristic way of being for that species is not a statistical notion, but rather a teleological notion, one that considers the function of that species and what is involved in being a good specimen of that species. As such it is compatible with the idea that many *actual* specimens of that species may fail to be *good* specimens of the species.

So much for teleology and nature, we will now move on to considering how we could interpret Aristotle to counter the direct arguments against teleology. While teleological arguments are attributed primarily to Aristotle, these types of arguments were present and defended well before his time, and in many ways Aristotle sought to revise how previous teleological arguments should be understood. Aristotle's predecessors often saw the use of goals and ends in nature as being brought about by a creator, but this is exactly the view of teleology that Aristotle sought to revise.

> Aristotle's radical alternative was to assert nature itself as an internal principle of change and an end, and his teleological explanations focus on the internal and intrinsic ends of natural substances – those ends that benefit the natural thing itself. To these he contrasted incidental ends of natural things, such as possible uses of the thing that do not serve its own functions and interests.[8]

Aristotelian teleology rather than being a theory outdated by our modern scientific understanding of nature, dependent on an external creator to generate causes, is in fact remarkably compatible with modern accounts of nature.

Aristotle gives an account of organs and beings by considering what something is for in terms of how it benefits the survival of that kind and what is necessary in order to achieve this aim. Aristotle points out that the organs of different animals differ because different animals have different modes of life and motion and therefore have different requirements for living these lives. For example, eyelids are necessary for birds in order to keep the eyes moist, eyes that are moist lead to more accurate vision, which in turn is necessary for creatures that hunt their prey on the earth from miles above in the sky. Fish, on the other hand, live in water and therefore have no need for eyelids at all.[9] This teleological account does not rely on a creator who gave birds eyelids but rather explains the organ by reference to the intrinsic ends of this species' nature.

> . . . Aristotle's explanations in this field (what we call ethology) conform to his general pronouncements that the activities of animals serve to support the primary functions of their souls, survival (nutrition and growth) and reproduction. In animals with greater capacities, the lower-level activities exist for the sake of the higher, such as perception, namely pleasure.[10]

Rather than being inimical to modern, evolutionary accounts of nature, Aristotle's teleology seems to foreshadow some of their more important insights.

Aristotle achieves this without placing humans at the centre of the natural stage and without making the ends of other species subsidiary to those of humans. The function of different organisms is the end that is intrinsic to that organism and cannot be an end which is instrumental to another organism. So while we can eat pigs and harvest their organs for our purposes, neither of these activities is the function of pigs *qua* pigs, as they are both incidental functions to the pigs' nature. '. . . that which is good in itself or by its own nature can only incidentally be good because of, or for the sake of something else'.[11] So, neither is Aristotelian teleology anthropocentric nor is there confusion in deciding which of the many different, possible functions of an organism is the organism's natural function. While it is possible to put organisms to other uses, their function is what is intrinsic to their own nature; it is derived from what the organism is like in itself.[12]

3. Moral luck

For Aristotle, the relationship between normativity and nature is not one of complete determination. As we saw previously, the function of humans is reason, so our ability to reason shapes and determines what the good life is for us. However, at the same time, our nature imposes some constraints on what is possible. Morality is neither entirely determined by our natures nor can it wholly escape our natures and operate in complete separation from what is natural for us *qua* human beings. Consider, for example, the consequentialist demand for impartial benevolence, the demand that one accept the claims of competing drowning babies equally, with no special weight to the fact that one of these babies is your child. The virtue ethicist would respond here that the demand for impartial benevolence frustrates natural human instincts to care for our own children.[13] These instincts exist for a good reason because they promote the survival of our species, and trying to overcome them would be both futile and counter-productive as it would lead to conceptions of moral demands that are at odds with what we are essentially like as a natural kind. Naturally, we are social creatures who benefit from contact with others of our species, naturally we feel empathy and concern towards others of our species and naturally we have strong protective instincts towards our own young. Our account of morality must embrace these facts about our nature or risk being irreparably distorted.

One consequence of these ideas is that the good life for human beings is therefore constrained by facts about our nature; we are naturally social animals so we have need of others to flourish, goods like friendship become essential to the good life, we have strong bonds to our children so we need our children to do well and be happy otherwise our well-being is severely affected, we have aims and goals so we need these aims and goals to not be affected by chronic pain, severe illnesses or life-shortening problems and so on. All this means that the good life for human beings is very vulnerable to luck and gives the Aristotelian a different perspective on the problem of moral luck.

The problem of moral luck was introduced to moral philosophy in its present form by Bernard Williams and Thomas Nagel. To understand moral luck, we need to think a bit about the relationship between morality and responsibility. Imagine that Ava punches Stephen, fully intending to cause him harm. She decides to punch him, forms a plan on how to go about it and carries out her plan successfully. In such a scenario, we would want to hold Ava morally responsible for what she has done. Imagine, however, a different scenario in which Ava gives Stephen an identical punch, causing him exactly the same amount of pain and harm, but this time she does so because she suffers from Tourette's syndrome. Due to her condition Ava is subject to uncontrollable arm movements and Stephen, who does not know this, comes up to her from behind so that he is inadvertently punched by one of her flaying arms. While the pain and harm caused in both scenarios is identical, it seems inappropriate to hold Ava *morally responsible* for her action in the second case. Although she is clearly causally responsible for Stephen's pain, the fact that she had no control over her actions, would, all other things being equal, absolve her of *moral* responsibility for them. That is, in the second case, we wouldn't want to blame her for what she did as we do not hold her responsible in the relevant way. These two scenarios bring out the connection between morality and control, that is, we generally only hold people morally responsible for acts that they had control over. Making judgements of responsibility, judgements of moral praise and blame, presupposes agency and voluntariness, that is, that this act originated in the agent in a way in which it is an expression of his agency. The problem of moral luck challenges this assumption about the necessary connection between morality, control and responsibility.

Cases of moral luck are paradoxical, they are cases where a significant element of the situation is outside of the agent's control; however, we still want to hold him morally responsible for it.[14] So we have lack of control as in the Tourette's case, which normally leads to absolving the agent of moral responsibility, but at the same time we still want to attribute moral praise or blame. Cases of moral luck then are cases of tension, unease, cases where we are not entirely certain that our judgements are merited. The problem of moral luck is best illustrated by example and the examples below correspond to the three kinds of moral luck identified by Nagel:

1   Two drivers go to their local pub fully intending to drink and not having made any alternative arrangements about how they will get home at the end of the night. They both get drunk and then drive home. Because they are drunk they both lose control of their vehicles and swerve onto the pavement; however, one is lucky in that there is no one about, he manages to swerve back onto the road and makes it home safely. The other drunk driver is less lucky; when he swerves onto the pavement, he hits and kills a pedestrian who happened to be there. This is a case of *resultant moral luck*, that is the results of one's actions are outside of the agent's control (whether there was one pedestrian, two pedestrians, a group of children or no one at all on the pavement at the time the car swerved onto it was not under the driver's control) but we still want to hold him morally responsible for what he did, that is, killed a pedestrian.

2   A German citizen decides to immigrate to Argentina in 1930 and as a result never has to face a difficult moral choice: had he stayed in Germany, would he have had the strength of character to stand up to the Nazis? Would he have been able to resist the peer pressure to conform to the ruling regime, would he have been able to stand up to the threats against non-conformists and speak out against a terrible evil? We will never know because he simply bypassed the entire moral test because he had already immigrated. Millions of fellow Germans failed the same test and responded with complicity and silence to the evils perpetrated by the Nazis, but perhaps the only thing that separates our immigrant from his fellow countrymen is his good luck in being in another country where he did not have to face the same moral test. *Situational moral luck* refers to the kinds of situations we come across which are outside our control but may still shape our characters, put us under pressure or tempt us to act immorally:

What we do is also limited by the opportunities and choices with which we are faced, and these are largely determined by factors beyond our control. Someone who was an officer in a concentration camp might have lead a quiet and harmless life if the Nazis had never come to power in Germany. And someone might have become an officer in a concentration camp if he had not left Germany for business reasons in 1930.[15]

3   Finally *constitutive moral luck* refers to the fact that who we are, the kinds of people we are including our natural inclinations, capacities and temperament are all out of our control but we are still praised for being kind and blamed for being cruel. We have no control over our natures, the fundamental strengths and weaknesses we are born with, but these go a long way towards shaping who we become.

These examples show how moral luck is an oxymoronic term, morality presupposes control, whereas luck is about lack of control and cases of moral luck are problematic because they bring the two together. There is a tension in all cases of moral luck. There is unease that the lucky drunk driver gets away without repercussions, there is a feeling of unfairness in the judgement of wrongdoing levelled against the German citizens who failed a test any of us would have also failed had we had to face it, there is an unease with the idea that we hold people morally responsible for natural tendencies that they merely had the good or bad luck to be born with. The problem of moral luck is characterized as a problem because it leaves us feeling that something should be done to either make the problem disappear or revise our judgements in light of it.

There are a number of possible responses to the problem of moral luck. As we saw in Part I, the Kantian emphasis on the purity of morality would mean that a Kantian would reject altogether the possibility of moral luck. He would base judgements of moral responsibility solely on the good will and not on its results, and he would expect the good will to overcome situational and constitutive factors. The good will is good without any qualifications, so the two drunken drivers are equally guilty for driving drunk and endangering the lives of others regardless of whether they hurt anyone or not, orienting oneself towards the moral law is a possibility at all times for all German citizens regardless of what moral tests they actually face and acting out of duty is a possibility for all of us regardless of our backgrounds.

The Aristotelian has a completely different approach to the problem of moral luck; it's less of a problem and more of a part of the human experience. Luck is part of the human condition, we are shaped by our nature and our development is affected by our environments. We cannot escape luck, but nor should we want to because luck is part of the human condition:

> That I am an agent, but also a plant; that much that I did not make goes towards making me whatever I shall be praised or blamed for being; that I must constantly choose among competing and apparently incommensurable goods and that circumstances may force me to a position in which I cannot help being false to something or doing some wrong that an event that simply happens to me may, without my consent, alter my life; that is equally problematic to entrust one's good to friends, lovers or country and to try to have a good life without them – all these I take to be not just the material of tragedy but everyday facts of lived practical reason.[16]

Reason must choose virtue, do so knowingly and do it for the sake of virtue, but that does not mean that reason has free reign irrespective of external influences. The moral life is like a delicate plant that requires care, favourable weather conditions, the right nutrients, etc. to flourish, but can be cut down by a storm, a drought or the wrong type of soil. Aristotle gives us the example of Priam, the legendary king of Troy, whose army is defeated, whose city is sacked, whose sons are killed and whose life is ruined through the loss of all the external goods that are necessary for the good life. Priam is less eudaimon because, through extreme bad luck, he has lost the ingredients necessary for the good life. The function of Priam's life was to govern and the loss of all these external goods means that he can no longer act virtuously at all, so luck has put an end to his eudaimonia. Virtue is a state of being expressed in action and while being prevented from acting once or twice has no effect on one's virtue, being entirely deprived of all the means for virtuous action does affect one's ability to be virtuous.

Constitutive and situational luck are embraced by Aristotelians. We are delicate creatures that lead fragile lives, in that our happiness cannot be guaranteed as it is situated in who we are and the world we live in. We have to accept that becoming moral is a sensitive enterprise, one that is vulnerable to all sorts of contingencies. There is unfairness in the way luck affects our lives, but a moral theory that can accommodate this offers a much more plausible picture of the kinds of lives beings like us live, than one which seeks to deny the influence of luck and tries to make us immune to all sorts of empirical factors that go towards making us who we are. The problem of moral luck is no longer a problem, but a correct account of what life is like for creatures like us.

Having said that, for Aristotle, reason plays a part in the moral life, so the drunk driver should have planned other options for getting home before he got drunk and in not doing so he displays the vice of callousness regardless of whether he actually killed anyone or not later on, but at the same time reason is not all powerful. Our natural constitutions, our environments, our family and friends play a huge role in who we become, but we have little or no control over such factors. This means that while situational and constitutive luck greatly influence our lives, resultant luck is less of a concern for the Aristotelian as agents are judged on their characters, not on the actions that proceed from them. We will return to these ideas in Chapter 7 when we consider the problem of weakness of the will, but for now we must conclude our discussion of teleology.

4. Hursthouse and Foot on teleology

Finally in this chapter on teleology, we will look at how modern virtue ethicists have developed naturalistic teleology beyond Aristotle's ideas. Hursthouse and Foot work very much in the same tradition and credit each other with inspiration, although Foot's naturalism is perhaps more radical than Hursthouse's.

According to Hursthouse, certain character traits are virtues because they make their possessor a good human being, a notion which is understood in terms of 'human nature, on what is involved in being good *qua* human being'.[17] The virtuous man recognizes the good life; however, what makes it the good life is not that it has been recognized by the virtuous man but rather because of the way it relates to human nature. Similarly, a good action and one's reasons for acting are not defined by what a virtuous person would do and his reasons but rather because they have a particular relationship to a naturalistic conception of flourishing. In this way, Hursthouse bypasses many of the objections we considered earlier on about the over-reliance of virtue ethics on the role of the virtuous person.[18]

As one would expect of a naturalistic account, what she has to say about humans is very similar to what she has to say about animals. All living things can be evaluated in the same way, that is, *qua* specimens of their natural kind. The more sophisticated animals can be evaluated with respect to four ends: individual survival, the continuance of the species, characteristic pleasure/freedom from pain and the good functioning of a social group. Exactly the same can be said of human beings, since we are part of the natural world as much as other animals; however, a significant addition in the human case is that our characteristic way of being[19] is the rational way. Humans are not merely pawns of nature, entirely determined by their natural constraints, but rather we are rational creatures, a fact which allows us to make choices and be held accountable for them.

The relationship between nature and reason though is different in Hursthouse than in Aristotle. Where for Aristotle nature it a constraint that could occasionally frustrate reason, for Hursthouse nature provides the raw materials that reason can shape into its own purpose. This is a stronger version of the role of reason and its ability to influence our human natures, but still a naturalistic account, one which looks to evaluate humans as part of the natural order. Rationality itself is the natural way of being for humans, not a statistical notion, but a normative one, '. . . our rationality makes us different from other living things, but is as much a natural fact about us and the world we live in as are facts about other species, and about us insofar as we are like them and our lives like theirs'.[20]

The other relevant point about Hursthouse's conception of rationality is that it allows for a wide and general account of the eudaimon life. There isn't just one, determinate and specific way to lead a flourishing life, rather we can each reason about what consists in the good life for us in our specific circumstances. The answer to what kind of life I should lead is an objective one but it is qualified in two ways: first it is contingent on facts about human nature and second it allows for different conceptions of the good life for different people in different circumstances.

Hursthouse's naturalism seeks to bridge the plausibility of a theory based on what we are like *qua* members of our species, with a robust conception of rationality that allows us to critically reflect on our choices. One of the concerns however with this account is why do we then come across so many humans who appear to be defective members of the species, that is, who fail to follow the dictates of rationality as based on our human nature? Why do most humans fail to act in accordance with the species' characteristic way of being? This is problematic both in terms of what other living creatures do – for example, wolves are not inundated with members who refuse to share the hunt with the pack, who fail to accept the pack hierarchy, who are defective as specimens of the species – as well as being problematic conceptually, for we would expect to see a preponderance of humans behaving in the way that is characteristic of the species. Either rationality is a natural characteristic of humans, but we would then expect to find most specimens of the kind conforming to the characteristic, or rationality is a normative concept which does not necessarily reflect the way people are and is therefore divorced from the naturalism that Hursthouse finds so attractive.

Foot also presents a naturalistic account of morality, similarly seeing virtues as those traits that enable human being to flourish and understanding what is involved in flourishing by reference to our particular natures as members of a natural kind. However, she also sees the virtues as traits that we *need* in order to fulfil our natural function; 'Anyone who thinks about it can see that for human beings the teaching and following of morality is something necessary. We can't get on without it'.[21] Virtues are necessary for human beings in the same way that other characteristics are necessary and other animals; 'Men need the virtues as bees need their stings',[22] Geach writes in the same vain as Foot. We need morality to function as human beings and this claim is based on what we are like as members of a natural kind.

The virtues are not only necessary for humans but also beneficial for their possessor:

> It seems clear that the virtues are, in some general way, beneficial. Humans do not get on very well without them. Nobody can get on well if he lacks courage, and does not have some measure

of temperance and wisdom, while communities where justice and charity are lacking are apt to be wretched places to live, as Russia was under Stalinist terror, or Sicily under the Mafia.[23]

The virtues are not merely instrumental for living the good life, they are constitutive of it. We come to evaluate human lives in the same way we evaluate animal and plant lives. When we apply the term 'good' to a human disposition, we are using it in the same way we apply the term 'good' to a root system. In the same way that a good root system is strong, robust and successful in providing nutrients to the tree, a good disposition is beneficial to the human who possesses it. What it is like to be a good human being derives from biological facts about what it is to be a human being.

One of the main problems with Foot's account is that it may be losing its grip on normativity. She establishes such a close connection between goodness and facts about our biological and zoological nature that it is unclear where the normativity of morality will emerge from. In a sense, this is a variant of the objection we saw above, namely that one cannot draw normative conclusions from descriptive facts. Moral facts have a feature that natural facts do not, that is, the force of morality, the power of the 'ought', and if we rely exclusively on natural facts, it is not clear how we will be able to draw normative conclusions. Humans look after their young, form social relations and mate for life; however, they also abuse their children, behave in antisocial ways and get divorced; which of these natural facts about the species should we focus on? It is not clear that behaving in antisocial ways is biologically inconsistent with being human, although we would still want to claim that it is immoral and wrong – on Foot's account it's not clear how we would be able to do so.

Further readings

Johnson, 2005 offers an excellent, detailed, book length account of the main objections against Aristotelian teleology and a superbly analytical defence against these objections on behalf of Aristotle. For critical accounts of teleology, see Kitcher, 1999 and Hull, in Hull and Ruse, 1998. For summary accounts of naturalism as an approach to ethical theory, see Buckle, in Singer, 1991, or Sturgeon, in Copp, 2006, or the very detailed Lenman, 2009, online.

The problem of moral luck was first presented in its current form to modern moral philosophy in the papers by Williams, and by Nagel, both reprinted in Statman, 1993, which has an excellent introduction by Statman on the problem of moral luck. In the same volume, Andre gives an Aristotelian's response to moral luck and for a book length discussion of Aristotle on moral luck see Athanassoulis, 2005.

Hursthouse's thoughts on naturalism form Part III of her 1999 book, while Foot's work can be found in her 1977 and her 2001 books. For a critical summary of the two theories, see Stohr and Wellman, 2002.

Conclusion for Part Two

The aim of this chapter has been to follow through the development of a particular kind on eudaimonistic virtue ethics. This is not the only version of virtue ethics in the literature but it is the one that has probably had the most impact in research in the area. Furthermore, not all authors discussed in these chapters would agree with all the interpretations as presented nor would they be willing to accept all the arguments, all the way through, as presented. Rather, this is an account of how a particular train of thought has developed because of the contributions of a variety of thinkers who have been influenced by each others' work. Fundamentally, this version of virtue ethics has its roots in Aristotle, although many of the ideas presented require the interpretation of original texts, while others take inspiration from Aristotelian ideas and develop them in new and novel directions.

We started off with an idea which has been fundamental in distinguishing virtue ethics from deontology and consequentialism, namely that the concept of 'virtue' has a primary role in virtue ethics. This was captured by two thoughts: that moral praise and blame are appropriate judgements of the agent's character and that the virtues are linked to human nature. We considered how praise for true virtue is only appropriate for actions that are chosen, chosen knowingly and chosen for their own sake, rather than actions that come about as a result of accidents, mistakes or non-virtue related motives.

We then looked at a detailed definition of virtue starting with Aristotle's function argument, that is, the argument that in order to find out the good life for human beings, we should ask what human beings are for, what is their function *qua* human beings. The function of humans turns out to be the ability to reason and the good life is the life in accordance with reason, that is, the life of virtue. Much of our understanding of virtue rested on the Doctrine of the Mean as a doctrine of appropriateness. The Doctrine suggests that feelings are parts of choices and actions, and must be displayed in the right amount, neither too much nor too little, but just right. The right amount of feeling to be displayed in virtue is relative to the individual and the circumstances and so cannot be known in advance of knowing the particulars of the situation.

Following on, we considered the role of the virtuous person and acknowledged a number of difficulties with the idea that we should apply directly to the virtuous person as a guide to virtue. Rather what we should take from the virtuous person is his ability to perceive the morally salient particulars of a situation and to apply practical wisdom to their evaluation. Both are abilities that take time and effort to develop, form part of the long process of Aristotelian character development, and both are abilities that involve intertwined reasoning and affective skills.

Finally, we returned to question the validity of the teleological approach, examining some of the criticisms that had led to its abandonment by modern moral philosophers, but then went on to offer possible replies to these problems through a reinterpretation of Aristotle. As part of this discussion, we considered the Aristotelian response to the problem of moral luck, seeing it less as a problem and more as a valuable part of the human experience. To conclude, we considered two new versions of naturalistic teleology to be found in the work of virtue ethicists Rosalind Hursthouse and Philippa Foot.

In Part III, we will cast a forward-looking glance at the future of virtue ethics. In Chapter 7, we will consider the virtue ethical response to the challenge presented by personality psychology and in doing so will try to account for why most people fail to be virtuous. In Chapter 8, we will look at some practical issues concerning professional education in the virtues. And finally in Chapter 9, we will consider how neo-Kantians have responded to the arguments put forward by virtue ethicists and how this dialogue has served to redefine both theories.

Current developments in virtue ethics

CHAPTER SEVEN

The challenge from personality psychology

1. The fundamental attribution error

In Part I of this volume, we looked at the work of a number of philosophers who were dissatisfied with the available options in modern moral philosophy and called for a radical change in the way we understand normative theories. The result was a group of theories that conceive of 'virtue' and 'character' as primary in their accounts of ethics. In Part II of this volume, we followed a particular train of thought that has developed into eudaimonistic virtue ethics. We saw how this approach has its routes in Aristotle's ethics, but also how new interpretations and new elements have been added in response to modern objections. In Part III, we will now consider current developments in virtue ethics and examine three distinct areas of interest. In this chapter, we will examine the challenge posed to virtue ethics from personality psychology[1] and, in responding to this challenge, we will get a better understanding of the practical impact of virtue ethics for people like us rather than for idealized perfectly virtuous agents. In Chapter 8, we will consider a practical issue: how should we go about educating for the virtues in the professions? Some professions, for example medicine, have a particular interest in instructing their students in the virtues and in this chapter we will consider practical problems with and solutions for educating for the virtues. Finally, in Chapter 9, we will look at how Kantians have responded to the criticisms levelled against their theory by virtue ethics, and how these responses have shaped the debate between the two alternatives. However, first we must see whether virtue ethics can meet the challenge from personality psychology.

Right at the start of the new millennium, just as virtue ethics was generally acknowledged as a viable alternative to other normative theories, two philosophers, Gilbert Harman and John Doris, came up, independently, with versions of an argument which claimed that empirical work from personality psychology showed that the conception of character which plays such a central role in virtue ethics simply does not exist in the case of Harman, or is fatally flawed in the case of Doris. We will examine the argument in detail and how it was presented slightly differently by the two philosophers, but fundamentally the claim is that philosophy as a discipline has been unaware of work that has taken place in another discipline, personality psychology, and that empirical results from personality psychology prove that there are no such things as character traits. If there are no such things as character traits, then ethical theories that rely on them to make sense of morality, most importantly virtue ethics, are in deep trouble as they rely on concepts that do not in fact exist. If true, this is an extremely serious challenge to virtue ethics as well as any other theory that relies on the concepts of 'character' or 'virtue'.

In this section, we will look at the challenge in detail, as presented by both Harman and Doris. In the next section, we will reconsider the empirical evidence the challenge relies on, suggesting that perhaps the evidence is less supportive of Harman's and Doris's cases than it would at first appear. In Section C, we will examine the main response from the virtue ethical camp, namely that the issue here is not the non-existence of character traits but their misidentification and the sensitivity of character development to situational factors. Finally in Section D, I will suggest that rather than posing a challenge to virtue ethics, evidence from personality psychology can be a rich ground for further philosophical reflection and is very much compatible with other virtue ethical claims.

Gilbert Harman's case against virtue ethics is a comprehensive one:

It seems that ordinary attributions of character traits to people are often deeply misguided and it may even be the case that there is no such thing as character, no ordinary character traits of the sort people think there are, none of the usual moral virtues and vices.[2]

This conclusion comes from a mistake we make called the fundamental attribution error. We tend to make all sorts of mistakes in our everyday reasoning. Faced with a fair coin that has come up heads five times in a row most people expect the sixth throw to produce tails as that result is 'overdue' (in fact, the chance of coming up tails remains the same as every other toss, 50:50). When assessing the risks of a surgery, we are more likely to go ahead if presented with the success rate rather than the failure rate (even though knowing one provides information about the other). In the Müller-Lyer optical illusion, two horizontal lines are identical in length but one appears much longer because of the direction the arrows point to at either end of the line. The lines continue to appear different to us even when we know they are the same length. If we make mistakes when we reason about risk or probabilities and even mistakes when faced with known optical illusions, perhaps we also make mistakes with how we think about other people's characters and that mistake is the fundamental attribution error. When we make the fundamental attribution error we attribute to others character traits that they don't actually have in the same way that we mistakenly assume that the coin is due to come up tails or assume that the success rate represents less of a risk than the failure rate.

We will consider two of the most famous experiments in personality psychology: first the Milgram experiments and then the Good Samaritan experiment. Imagine Adam and Bob both volunteer to take part in an experiment about learning and how pain affects one's ability to get the answer right. Adam is the 'questioner', he asks a series of questions which Bob has to answer. If Bob gets the answer right, Adam moves onto the next one, however if Bob gets the answer wrong, Adam administers an electric shock which gets progressively stronger. Bob is strapped in to the electric shock machine next door, but Adam can see him through a mirror. Unfortunately, Bob is not very good at this test and keeps getting the answers wrong. Adam keeps shocking him, but as the level of the shocks increases Bob becomes increasingly uncomfortable, then vocal and unhappy about the experiment, then apparently more and more in pain. Adam is encouraged to continue shocking Bob by the experimenter who is also present in the room. However, this experiment is a trick, it is a trick played on Adam. Bob is not a volunteer, but an actor, he is not receiving electric shocks; he is merely pretending to be in pain. This is not an experiment about learning rather it is a test to see how far Adam is willing to go on shocking Bob just because he is told he must do so by the experimenter.

The experiment was designed with the after effects of the World War II in mind. During the Nuremburg trials, a number of defendants argued that what they did in torturing and killing millions of prisoners might have been wrong but they were absolved of responsibility for it because they were simply following orders. The Courts rejected this defence on the grounds that we ought to stand up to authority and refuse to do things we know are morally abhorrent. The Courts assumed that simply being told by someone in authority to do something immoral is no excuse for obedience and most people would know this and refuse. The Milgram experiments were set up to confirm this conclusion, that is, that most people would refuse to act immorally simply because they were told to, but in fact the experiments seem to prove the opposite. While 100% of people predicted in advance that they would refuse to obey authority in situations in which they were ordered to act immorally, only 40% in fact stopped shocking Bob. Up to 60% of people in Adam's position were willing to continue shocking Bob even when he was in very evident distress, and even when the electric shock machine dials indicated he was receiving a shock capable of causing serious harm or death. Participants were far more willing to continue shocking when encouraged to do so by someone in authority, and their behaviour was affected by surprising factors, for example, whether the experimenter was male or female, wearing a white coat or not, and carrying a clip board or not (as it turns out, white coat wearing, clip board carrying males are perceived as the most authoritative).

While the Milgram experiments tempt subjects to act immorally by getting someone in authority to prompt them to do so, the Good Samaritan experiment places subjects under pressure in a situation where inaction is immoral. In the Good Samaritan experiment, students training to become priests are asked to prepare a lecture on the Biblical Good Samaritan parable (the Good Samaritan being the only person who stopped to help a stranger in need while others walked on by). The students are told that they are running late and asked to hurry to the lecture theatre. On the way to the lecture theatre they come across a person who appears to be in some kind of distress at the side of the road. This time the injured person is the actor and is placed there to see whether the rushing students will stop and *be* the Good Samaritan or continue on their way to merely *talk* about the Good Samaritan. Again, the large majority of students failed to stop and help.

According to Harman, these experiments show that although we assume that we and other people are kind and helpful, we are mistaken, we attribute to ourselves and to others character traits that in fact do not exist – we make the fundamental attribution error.

Doris's[3] argument is different from Harman's but has similar conclusions, namely that behavioural reliability (i.e. stable character traits that result in reliable behaviours), which is central to the theoretical understanding of virtue ethics, is not backed up by the empirical observation of behaviour undertaken in personality psychology. Doris points out that virtue ethics postulates the existence of structured, reliable behaviours, that is, character traits that are stable, predictable and exhibited over time; however, this is not the case in practice. Doris does not go as far as Harman in doubting the very existence of character traits, but he does claim that the empirical evidence argues against the Aristotelian conception of character traits as robust dispositions. Doris' argument has four lines of attack. First, he argues that differences in behaviour in a population are the result of situational differences rather than dispositional differences as virtue ethics would have us believe; it's not our characters that differ but the situations we come across. So, for example, the reason why A behaved dishonestly at time t, was because he was tempted by the presence of the loose change rather than because he is dishonest as opposed to the honest majority; honesty and dishonesty do not exist as character traits. Second, even when behaviour does appear reliable, this can easily be challenged by introducing situational variation. Ultimately, behaviour may only appear reliable because situations and contexts tend to be similar, so we all tend to come across the same situations and therefore appear to have stable responses to them. Third, individuals are not evaluatively consistent, for example, some Nazis exhibited both brutality towards certain people and at the same time compassion towards other people or towards animals, so they were both brutal and kind at different times. Finally, Doris points out that people possess many more traits than those traditionally identified by some virtue ethicists (including Aristotle himself).[4] Fatally for a theory which claims to put forward a more plausible conception of moral psychology than its rivals, virtue ethics seems to ignore the findings of personality psychology.

This is the case against virtue ethics. In the following section, we will cast a critical look at the evidence that gives rise to the objection, while in Sections C and D, we will consider whether virtue ethics can in fact accommodate the conclusions of personality psychology rather than be challenged by them.

2. Reconsidering the empirical evidence

I am not an expert in personality psychology, but if the conclusions of another discipline are to be applied to philosophy, then there is some obligation on philosophers to become familiar with these conclusions in their entirety, by which I mean that we should be familiar with all discussions of these conclusions in the other discipline and not merely the ones that appear to support our case. So what is personality psychology, what do the experiments show and how should their conclusions be interpreted?

Personality psychology is the study of individuality. It concerns itself with processes in individuals which are responsible for resulting behaviour. The study of personality relies on measurements of behaviours, such as correlations between different characteristics.[5] A significant area of debate in personality psychology has focused over the question of the existence of traits. The once dominant approach of assuming that dispositions are fundamental to personality has been challenged by a series of experiments.[6] Unfortunately, the experiments providing this empirical data are limited, as, by their very nature, they are problematic. It is essential to these experiments that the subject is deceived as to the true aim of the exercise (and, as an aside, because of this they raise serious ethical questions concerning the permissibility of conducting research without valid consent, concerning the risks of exposing subjects to gravely stressful situations and concerning the problems with revealing to unwitting subjects that they may be a lot less moral than they thought. These ethical concerns make the replication of such experiments all but impossible nowadays[7]). Doris has raised concern with the limited number of experiments philosophers appear familiar with,[8] so it is worth trying to refer to as many of the analyses of the experiments as possible, as well as the two main experiments we outlined above.

The experiments were conducted within a theoretical background which assumed that there are internalized behavioural dispositions, and that these dispositions manifest themselves independently of situational factors.[9] The experiments were designed to test whether traits could be successfully used as behaviour predictors. So, the first question we need to answer is, what did these experiments show? The experiments are claimed to have illustrated a number of points, these are discussed below in no particular order:

1   The prevalence of immorality: The experiments are surprising in that they illustrate a greater degree of immoral behaviour than would have otherwise been expected (from asking potential participants to predict their own behaviour). The results surprised the researchers themselves in this respect, with Milgram writing 'What is surprising is how far ordinary individuals will go in complying with the experimenter's instructions. . .It is the extreme willingness of adults to go to almost any lengths on the command of an authority that constitutes the chief finding of the study and the fact most urgently demanding explanation'.[10]

2   Unpredictability of behaviour: Closely related to this idea is the psychological claim of the experimenters that we cannot predict behaviour from the ascription of traits to individuals.[11]

3   Inferring traits from single instances: Another result of the experiments was to cast doubt on the theoretical claim that one could infer the existence of traits from single instances.[12]

4   Limited cross-situational consistency: This is the claim that traits are not exhibited reliably in different situations.[13]

5   The importance of situational factors: Related, but distinct from the above point, this is the claim that situational rather than dispositional factors are more likely to account for variations in behaviour, so that '[d]isruption in habitual role behaviours and environmental relations can alter even long-standing personality patterns'.[14]

These claims are made by the psychologists who carried out these experiments and those who have since analysed their work. Harman's critique does not make explicit reference to these claims as such but rather takes it more or less as granted that personality psychology *has* illustrated that there are no such things as character traits. However, as will become evident, the claims are more complex than Harman's conclusion, which is the reason why they are presented here in detail. Doris' account is more sensitive and makes use of the fourth and fifth claims, as well as the second claim which he relates to the unpredictability of behaviour. Here, it is interesting to note the ease with which philosophers appeal only to the claims which further their argument, making no reference to the rest. Claim three is never mentioned, although in personality psychology this has generated the greatest amount of controversy, with discussions focusing on the importance of aggregating as opposed to relying on single instances of behaviour (on this point see below). As an aside, we should be apprehensive of arguments that rely on 'picking' evidence from another discipline and presenting it out of context as such a practice risks highlighting only evidence which promotes one's case and does not fairly reflect the level of dissent on the issue within the originating discipline.

There are number of points that should be raised in relation to the empirical evidence itself and how it has been received within its own discipline. The first point is that the experiments involve very complex interpretations of data and there is some dispute in the literature as to how the data should be interpreted and what it purports to show.[15] Having an opinion on this debate, let alone resolving it, requires an extensive knowledge of statistics, which I thoroughly lack; however, it is worth noting that there is a debate within the discipline itself about how the data should be interpreted. Similarly, there is discussion about the main conclusion, that is, that traits cannot be used as behaviour predictors. Epstein points out that although traits cannot predict *single* instances of behaviour, as dispositions they are useful when aggregating the same act over occasions,[16] so that '. . .behaviour is simultaneously situationally specific and unstable at the individual level and general and stable at the aggregate level'.[17] Furthermore, the conclusions of some of the experiments themselves have to be interpreted with caution. One of the conclusions of the Good Samaritan experiment was that '. . .whether a person helps or not is an instant decision likely to be situationally controlled. How a person helps involves a more complex and considered number of decisions, including the time and scope to permit personality characteristics to shape them',[18] which seems a much more subtle conclusion than the blanket claim that traits do not exist. It also seems to suggest that even the experimenters themselves acknowledge the influence of situational factors on how our character traits express themselves.

Another interesting point to note about the evidence is that not all experiments in this area of personality psychology that are implicitly cited in this debate are of relevance to moral philosophy as some are set up to measure morally neutral behaviours. Some studies were set up to discover whether traits such as extraversion, expressive movements and punctuality could be consistently identified in behaviour, but it is unclear what relevance such results would have for a theory of morally right and wrong action.[19] Finally, some of the relevant studies, that is, ones that did test plausibly moral traits, were conducted on children. For example, Hartshorne and May's study on honesty and resistance to temptation was conducted on 8,000 children[20]; the significance of this point should become evident below.

It seems then that the claims of personality psychologists themselves are both more modest than how they have been interpreted by some philosophers, for example, Harman, and more detailed and comprehensive than how they have been appealed to by others, for example, Doris. Also, there is significant debate within the discipline as to how this evidence should be interpreted in the first place and exactly what it shows at the individual and aggregate levels. And finally, some of the experiments are of doubtful relevance to philosophy as they examine morally neutral behaviours, while others draw conclusions about children, which, as we shall see, are a special case.

3. Weakness of will

The previous section cast some doubt on the interpretation of the empirical evidence the Harman/Doris critique of virtue ethics relies on from within personality psychology itself, but let us now assume that the evidence does indeed fully support the conclusions 1–5 above and see if virtue ethics may still have a response to these points.

Harman views character traits as 'relatively long-term stable dispositions to act in distinctive ways'[21] and we have to agree that virtues are indeed such character traits. It is also plausible to assume that one's character is exhibited in one's actions, as we have accounted for character as a state of being expressed in doing; however, the relation between character and action is a complex one. Character manifests itself in action, in that being in a virtuous state of character will lead one to act virtuously; however, action is not all that there is to someone's character in this sense. Actions are merely external manifestations of internal states and an inference is required before we can make judgements about the character from which the actions resulted. For example, in my role as a conscientious teacher, I call upon a shy student to present her work to the class. This is perceived by all present and the student herself, as an act of kindness showing the attention to individual needs required in teaching, as I am allowing the student special time to present her work, while others are kept quiet and attentive. It turns out that my student greatly benefits from the experience, gaining in confidence and attributing this gain to my skills as a teacher. However, unknown to all observers, my act was motivated by a desire to humiliate the student. Unfortunately for me, and against all my expectations, my act backfired and failed to reach its vicious aim. To the casual observer, my act is evidence of my kind and considerate character; however, knowledge of my inner state reveals me to be a mean, spiteful person, albeit rather incompetent in carrying out my spite. As we have seen previously, doing the right thing is not enough for virtue, one must do the right thing for the right reason and with the right desire, and here is an example where someone merely appears to be doing the right thing without being virtuous. However, as external observers of someone's character, all we have access to is the person's actions.

The personality psychology experiments only reveal evidence of the subjects' behaviour; the researchers then have to work hard to explain what this behaviour means in terms of the person's whole character. The second conclusion drawn from the experiments was that we cannot predict behaviour from the ascription of traits to individuals. However, we ascribe traits to individuals in the first place by drawing inferences from their behaviour, and these inferences are very vulnerable to error as the only evidence of the person's character we have in the first place is the behaviour we observe. If my students concluded from the example above that I am a kind and caring teaching, they would be making a mistake, but they would nonetheless be very surprised to see me act callously and spitefully the next time I taught them because they would not be aware of their own error about my character. If we recognize that our initial ascription of traits must be tentative, due to the difficulty of drawing inferences about one's character from one's behaviour in the first place, then we should not be surprised that future behaviours do not conform to what we expected. Character trait ascription is a difficult business, and we should expect to get it wrong.

Indeed, we are often tentative about the ascription of character traits and only do so for people we are intimately familiar with. We will only vouch for the characters of those we know well, the people we know over a long period of time, those whom we have seen act in a variety of circumstances, those whom we can say with confidence that we have seen repeated evidence of their character in their actions, for example, our friends, our family, etc. This idea casts doubt on whether the third conclusion of the experiments poses a threat to virtue ethics. The third conclusion was that one cannot infer the existence of traits from single instances; however, this is not part of the Aristotelian project in the first place. No account of virtue ethics expects us to be able to make character evaluations from single instances of behaviour. We need to observe a person's character over a long period of time and indeed Aristotle even seems to suggest that a person cannot be judged to have led a eudaimon life until that life is over[22] – a rather long time indeed, with plenty of opportunities for observing that person's character in action.

One possible worry here is that the researchers asked subjects to predict their own behaviour, and since we have access to our inner states, there should be a higher degree of reliability in predicting our own behaviour. However, knowledge of one's own self, especially when it comes to one's moral strength, is a very difficult thing. We would generally like to think well of ourselves and are optimistic about our chances of doing the right thing but we are often mistaken – that is the correct conclusion of the experiments. This conclusion is also a very interesting one for both psychologists and philosophers to consider further. Why do we find it difficult to correctly assess our own moral strength? Why do we tend to err on the side of virtue in assuming the best of ourselves? These are interesting questions that require further thought, but unfortunately we have to set them aside for our purposes here.

Another very important point is that character evaluation requires not just observation of the agent in action and observation of the agent in action over time but also observation of the agent in action in different circumstances and, in particular, under circumstances that are likely to tempt or pressure the agent into acting immorally. The experiments don't represent just any, random, kind of situation, but rather *specific* situations, purposefully engineered to put subjects under pressure or temptation to act immorally. To understand why so many people gave into these pressures and temptations, we need to consider Aristotle's account of all character traits not merely virtue.

Aristotle identified four character traits[23]: virtue, continence, incontinence and vice. Virtue and vice are similar because they are both stable, long-term, predictable and reliable character traits of the kind that Harman has in mind; although of course virtue chooses the good and vice chooses evil. Continence and incontinence differ from virtue and vice in this respect as they are both in a state of flux. We have seen how we are all born with certain natural tendencies and we have claimed that virtue is a stable character trait, so it is reasonable to ask: how does one get from natural tendencies to full virtue? There seem to be two possibilities: either there is some kind of instantaneous transformation from natural tendencies to fully settled virtue or the process is gradual. If virtue ethics suggested the instantaneous transformation option from natural tendencies to full virtue, I think there would be grounds for a serious objection here, as such an account seems deeply implausible when we look at human nature. However, as we have seen earlier, virtue ethics clearly argues for the second option: the move towards virtue is a gradual, slow change, which happens over a long period of time and is very vulnerable to external factors.

We all start off with certain natural tendencies which are then shaped by external factors and in this long process we fluctuate between continence and incontinence with respect to different virtues. The states of continence and incontinence are unlike the states of virtue and vice in that they are not stable and reliable, but rather they are, definitionally, flexible, interchangeable and shaped by situational factors. This is because continence and incontinence represent moral progression; they are states *we go through* on our way to virtue. Virtue, continence and incontinence all have some-thing in common: unlike vice, they all aim at the good. However, unlike the virtuous agent, the continent and incontinent agents are plagued by desires contrary to the right reason; they are both tempted, they both have to fight a struggle between their reason and their desires. The continent agent wins this struggle and does the right thing, so externally his behaviour is indistinguishable from that of the virtuous agent; however, whereas the virtuous agent's character flows smoothly and effortlessly into action because his desires are in line with his reason, the continent agent has to struggle to do what he knows is right. The incontinent agent loses this struggle and does the wrong thing, as his desires overwhelm his reason.

The best way to understand this progress is by example. I will give you a personal example, but if you can try and identify some aspect of your own character development that fits in with this account, you may find it will make more sense. When I was young I coveted my mother's fur coats. I thought they were the most beautiful, soft, luxurious coats ever and I couldn't wait to be old enough to own one (or many!). My state at the time was probably best described as a state of ignorance as I knew nothing about fur coats and where they came from. I was then shown a video at school explaining where fur came from, complete with baby seals being clubbed to death and all the gory details of the fur trade. Having found out where fur came from and what was involved in producing the coats I knew that I should no longer desire them, but this did not make the desire go away. I was now in a position where I could end up being either continent or incontinent. Faced with a beautiful fur coat and the money to buy it, it was a toss-up whether I would be able to withstand my desire to own it or not. If I bought the coat, I would be incontinent; if I walked away I would be continent. My will was weak; I knew the right thing to do, that is, not buy the fur coat, but my contrary desires resisted my reason. However, over time, my desires had a chance to be shaped by my reason. The more I learnt about the fur trade, the more I came across the animals that were used for the trade, the more I saw how the fur was procured, the more I was moved to think differently about fur coats. Now fur coats no longer look luxurious, soft and desirable. They look like the pain and suffering that has been involved in producing them and therefore are no longer desirable. Walking away from a fur coat sale is no longer a struggle as I do not wish to own something that was produced by so much suffering; my desires are now in line with my reasoning and flow smoothly into action.

The important point is that all this was a gradual move towards virtue, characterized by different approaches at different stages. Had you tempted me with a fur coat early on in my development, I would have failed the test. Had you tempted me with a fur coat on a bad day, on a day when I was sad or less able to resist temptation, I would have failed. Similarly, if we tempt people with immorality, they are much more likely to fail the test, and if we put obstacles in their way, they are more likely to stumble across them. The participants in the Milgram and Good Samaritan experiments were, for the most part, people who, like most of us, struggle to do good. On some days they succeed, but tempt them or pressure them to extremes and they are likely to fail. What we are seeing in these experiments are not people who were mistakenly thought to be virtuous but are indeed vicious, but rather people who drift between continence (right action) and incontinence (wrong action) in their struggle for moral maturity and stability. It is also important to truly appreciate that character development is a life-long process, as this insight has significant implications for the formation of empirical experiments. The Hartshorne and May study into character was conducted on children and this in itself is problematic. Character development is not a phase exclusive to childhood, it continues throughout one's life, nor is it a process that we can expect to record in a matter of days, weeks or months. To observe character changes, we need to not only observe individuals in many different types of situations but also over very long periods of time – this raises serious questions about the methodology of the experiments in personality psychology.

So while the ultimate goal, virtue, is a stable, predicable and reliable character trait, the road to virtue is nothing but. This explains claim four, the limited cross-situational consistency. Traits are not exhibited reliably in different situations because *the situations* affect the person's ability to exhibit the trait. Temptation, pressure, duress, distraction, etc. are all likely to divert people from the path to virtue. We can also account for the fifth claim, the importance of situational factors. Situational factors are indeed important, but they are important because they shape dispositional factors. The German who stays in Nazi Germany and fails the moral test will find his character shaped by the experience. It is not the case that situations affect what we do, while character traits do not exist, but rather that situations affect our characters which in turn result in different behaviours.[24] Virtue ethics has claimed so all along, so rather than being contrary to virtue ethics, the conclusions of the experiments are entirely consistent with the theory.

Finally we need to account for the first conclusion, the prevalence of immorality. Virtue ethics can explain this conclusion because what we are observing are imperfectly virtuous agents struggling with demanding and challenging moral tests. The experiments are examples of weakness of will, agents struggling and often failing to act morally under difficult circumstances. What is interesting about the experiments is not the *prevalence* of immorality but the *diversity* of immorality. Aristotle warned us that there are many ways to go wrong[25] and the experiments highlight these ways of getting it wrong.

4. Getting it wrong

One of the most interesting aspects of these experiments is that they confirm the Aristotelian claim that there are many ways of getting morality wrong. Rather than presenting a challenge to virtue ethics, these experiments are a rich source of materials confirming virtue ethics and giving practical illustrations of the theory's claims. It is beyond the scope of this chapter to give a full account of all the aspects of the experiments and their relevance to virtue ethics, but as this is a significant point, I will use the remainder of this chapter to partly illustrate this claim.

We saw earlier that the acquisition of virtue is a gradual process. Not only does developing a moral character take time but the process is dependent on the availability and quality of a number of factors. The presence of role models, good education, practices which assist in the habituation in the virtues, favourable peer influence, etc. can all go towards making us virtuous. We should not be surprised then that empirical experiments arrive at similar conclusions. The Hartshorne and May studies of honesty and deception in children concluded that honesty

> 'goes by gangs and classrooms' that 'a pupil resembles his friends in his tendency to deceive', that it occurs less often when an atmosphere of cooperation and good will is established between

teachers and friends. . .To instill honesty, they recommended
training in behaviours 'characterised by integrity of performance
and intelligent grasp of the social significance of honour'.[26]

Not only do the researchers in this study recognize the influence
of the environment in the development of both virtue and vice but
they also recommend developing appropriate habits on the road
to virtue. Notice also that the final recommendation incorporates
two significant elements of virtue ethics. Although good habits are
essential in the development of virtue, virtue is more than habituation.
Actual virtue involves knowledge and choice, which is significantly
more than an action performed out of habit. Hartshorne and May
recognize that training in habits of honesty and integrity is a part
of moral development, but they recommend that it is accompanied
by a deeper understanding of why honour is valuable and what it
demands of us. Here is advice to not only develop virtue through
habit but also develop real understanding of what virtue is and what
it requires of us, so that what was a habitual act can eventually
be affirmed as an act of virtue. Effectively Hartshorne and May
are recognizing the importance of moving from 'the that' to 'the
because' that we discussed in Chapter 3 section C.

Furthermore, one should not underestimate the complexity of the
conclusions of these experiments. Some commentators relating
the experiments rather simplify these conclusions, suggesting that
the experimenters expected to find generalized behavioural patterns
for specific behaviours (often those associated with positive traits
or virtues) and instead found that behaviour could be unexpectedly
(and often negatively) influenced by situational elements. However,
the conclusions of the experiments showed a much deeper and
more sensitive approach to understanding human behaviour. When
faced with a morally demanding situation, subjects may display
virtue or vice but more often they may well be confused about
what is required of them, may be torn between conflicting moral
obligations, may be victims of weakness of will or have accounts
of morality which place more emphasis on internal states (such as
intentions) rather than their external manifestation in actions. Here
are some examples of the above from the experiments.

Darley and Batson report of the Good Samaritan subjects that
they were 'in conflict between stopping to help the victim and
continuing on his way to help the experimenter. . .Conflict, rather

than callousness, can explain their failure to stop'.[27] These are not people who are, strictly speaking, immoral, but people who are challenged by the situation and confused as to what the right thing to do might be. Milgram reports numerous cases of weakness of will concluding that '[m]any people were unable to realize their values in action and found themselves continuing in the experiment even though they disagreed with what they were doing'[28] and '[s]ome subjects were totally convinced of the wrongness of what they were doing but could not bring themselves to make an open break with authority'.[29] While other subjects would characterize their behaviour as wrong, Milgram again reports that some subjects 'derived satisfaction from their thoughts and felt that – within themselves, at least – they had been on the side of angels'.[30]

Furthermore, the experiments reinforce Aristotelian claims about the appropriateness of behaviour and in particular the claims of the Doctrine of the Mean that the right action involves neither too much nor too little emotion we considered in Chapter 4 Section D. In a little discussed passage, Darley and Batson expand on the behaviour of those, few, subjects who did stop to help. Curiously, the mode of helping itself raises a number of interesting considerations. They identified two approaches among those who stopped to help: one style of helping was responsive to the 'victim's' needs and expressed wishes about the amount and type of help they needed. However, there was another style of helping with subjects directing their actions towards the presumed underlying needs of the 'victim'. This mode of helping was little modified by the 'victim's' own wishes, even to the point where 'victims' worried by the possible approach of the next experimental subject could not persuade the current subject to leave them alone. This may well be an instance of misidentified response and an example of vice at the other end of the scale. If not helping at all is clearly a vice, then, perhaps, helping beyond what is needed to the point of encroaching on another's wishes and autonomy is the other vice of excess and a good example of the Doctrine of the Mean in action.

Rather than posing a challenge for virtue ethics then, the empirical conclusions of the personality psychology experiments are perfectly compatible with the theory and even illustrate important aspects of virtue ethics. Virtue ethics has nothing to fear from this work; rather, philosophers should work closer with psychologists to confirm the many points of agreement.

Further readings

The case against virtue ethics is made in Harman, 1998–9, and various works by Doris, 1998, and 2002 and in Doris and Stich, in Smith and Jackson, 2005.

In this chapter, I have argued that true virtue is rare and this response with respect to personality psychology is defended in Annas, 2003, online, Athanassoulis, 2000, Kupperman, 2001, and DePaul, 1999, while Kamtekar, 2004, also develops an Aristotelian response to the challenge.

The account of weakness of will on which this position relies on is developed by McDowell, 1996b, in Lovibond and Williams.

There have been a number of other responses to the challenge from personality psychology, indicatively: Sreenivasan, 2002, comprehensively questions the interpretation of the experimental data and Montmarquet, 2003, challenges the validity of the experimental conclusions. Another account of virtue ethics which is compatible with the results of the experiments is Merritt's Humean inspired virtue ethics, in Merritt, 2000.

CHAPTER EIGHT

Moral education and
the virtues

1. Failing to notice

So far then I have developed and relied upon a particular account of virtue ethics, one that sees the perfectly virtuous agent as a rather rare phenomenon, and characterizes most of us as struggling on the long road to virtue, oscillating between continence and incontinence on different occasions and with respect to different virtues. Doris considers the virtue ethical response I have developed so far, that is, the claim that the virtues are rare, but worries that such a response robs Aristotelianism of its traditional appeal, that is, its appeal based on the promise of an engaging and lifelike moral psychology.[1] He wonders how reflection on a few gifted individuals can facilitate moral behaviour and how such a theoretically construed project could possibly fulfil Aristotle's aim of engaging in a practical enquiry. I have indeed presented an account of virtue ethics according to which the virtuous agent is a rare find, but as we saw in Chapter 5 this doesn't prevent us from making use of the concept. What we should be interested in is not what the virtuous agent might actually do but *how* he thinks and how to develop the moral perception and practical wisdom necessary for virtue.

Doris is concerned that '. . . if virtue is *expected* to be rare, it is not obvious what role virtue theory could have in a (generally applicable) programme of moral education',[2] unless one subscribes to a very elitist account of virtue according to which only the very few are entitled to a moral education. However, moral education does not pose a problem for virtue ethics and if anything this is more of a concern for a position like the one held by Doris. According to Doris, it is situational factors that influence behaviour, not dispositional ones. If that were true, it would be very difficult to see any role for moral education at all. All we would need is a lot of luck to avoid the situational factors that lead to the wrong behaviour and a lot of luck to come across the situational factors that lead to the right behaviour. Since the circumstances we come across, for example, whether we are tempted, or pressured or in a hurry, etc., cannot be affected by education, according to this account, luck is the only thing we can 'rely' on to produce good behaviour. In contrast, because virtue ethics allows that situational factors may shape dispositional traits, there is a role for education, since once these dispositional traits are correctly shaped by the right situational factors which include the right education, they can result in the right action. This account of virtue ethics places an enormous emphasis on moral education as this is what stands between us and the vicissitudes of the world. Our only hope to withstand situational factors is to have the moral maturity and strength that comes through a long and gradual process of moral development.[3]

Taking a cue then from Doris' concerns about the role of moral education in this version of virtue ethics, in this chapter we will look at some practical considerations concerning character development and we will reflect on what might be involved in moral education if we assume an account of the ideally virtuous agent as a rare individual who is more of an example of *how* to think rather than of *what* to think. In doing so, we will keep making some references back to the experiments we considered in the last chapter as they remain a rich source of inspiration. Another point of reference for this chapter will be examples from actual students of morality from my own experience, and that of other teachers, of teaching non-philosophy students ethics at the Higher Education level.

To start then, we should return to the most basic part of ethical decision making: noticing that a situation requires our moral attention in the first place. There are many ways in which we might fail to notice a situation. For example, some participants in the Good Samaritan experiment report entirely failing to notice the person in need – they just did not see him. This seems entirely plausible, especially since the seminaries were in a hurry and their attention was diverted elsewhere. Provided this failure is non-culpable, this kind of case absolves the subject from responsibility for failing to act morally because he simply was not aware that there was a situation which required this kind of response. However, there is a more interesting sense in which people 'fail to notice'; although they are aware of the situation, they fail to notice that it has *moral* significance. This is not a matter of being perplexed about what to do, but a more basic issue of failing to notice that there is a *moral question* in front of you. Consider this account of the subjects' recollections from the Good Samaritan example:

> Our seminaries in a hurry noticed the victim in that in the postexperimental interview almost all mentioned him as, on reflection, possibly in need of help. But it seems that they often had not worked this out when they were near the victim. Either the interpretation of their visual picture as a person in distress or the empathic reactions usually associated with that interpretation had been deferred because they were hurrying. According to the reflections of some of the subjects, it would be inaccurate to say that they realized the victim's possible distress, then chose to ignore it; instead, because of the time pressures, they did not perceive the scene in the alley as an occasion for an ethical decision.[4]

The subjects entirely failed to perceive what they were seeing as a moral situation, as a situation that in some way involved them in a moral question. They didn't altogether fail to see the victim in need, prostrate on the ground, but they failed to see the moral significance of this fact, they failed to perceive the situation as one which required their moral involvement. Morality is demanding, it asks questions of us, it involves in the world around us, so how is it possible that these seminaries entirely missed the point?

Even worse, the failure of the Seminaries is not an altogether rare, one-off occurrence. In my years teaching ethics to medical students, I have realized that one of the most important steps in their education is to try to sensitize them to the situations they came across. Medical students tend to be extremely intelligent, high-achieving students, capable of academic excellence in a variety of subjects, with a strong interest in pursuing medicine, so their failure to perceive moral situations isn't a matter of lack of intelligence or lack of interest. At the same time, medical practice abounds with moral questions, dealing as it does with vulnerable people who have to make very difficult decisions, so their failure to perceive moral situations is not down to the rarity of the moral situations either. Despite the availability of morally sensitive situations and the fact that the students are bright, motivated and interested, the students often fail to notice morality in practice.

Consider the following real example: a group of fourth year students were following a ward round. During ward rounds, students get to observe clinician/patient interactions and then discuss any issues that may have been raised during their round in a special seminar with their tutor. Given the nature of this teaching, nobody knows in advance what kinds of issues may crop up, but the students are asked to look out for not only clinical details but also make observations relating to communication skills, team work, social and cultural issues, etc. The students are not asked any questions during the rounds, they are not examined or put under any pressure to react to what they see – they are passive observers. In one of these sessions, a group of six students observed a teenage girl who was refusing treatment being physically restrained by three nurses; while treatment was being administered, the patient proceeded to scream and try to free herself from the restraints. In the seminar that followed the tutor asked whether the students had observed anything of interest in the round and no one could think of anything. She then asked specifically whether the students noticed anything of ethical importance but again no one could think of anything significant they might have seen. The tutor was extremely surprised as in her opinion the forced treatment of the teenager raised a number of ethical questions. It is important to note that the students were genuinely unable to recall the case as ethically important, as opposed to being reluctant to do so for fear of censure or out of timidity or out of a worry that they may be penalized. When the tutor presented the case to them as an ethical dilemma, they were all able to see that a serious moral question had been raised.[5]

How is it possible for these well-meaning, intelligent and motivated medical students to somehow miss the fact that they were witnessing a morally relevant situation? I think the answer lies with the fact that moral questions do not always occur spontaneously to people nor is morality in action immediately evident to everyone.

When I start my moral philosophy classes, I tell my students that they should expect this class to change their lives. This may sound pretentious, but why shouldn't it be true? Why shouldn't a class that asks 'What is the right thing to do?', 'What kind of person should I be?', 'How should I live my life?' not lead the students who take it to reconsider their own actions, their own characters and their own lives? To the contrary, it would be peculiar if the class failed to have any kind of practical impact on the students because morality is not an abstract topic solely relevant to passing exams, but a practical pursuit, central to everyone's lives. The practical impact I expect my teaching to have on my students is not a matter of indoctrination, I am not aiming to recruit them to any one particular moral view or pass on particular answers to ethical problems. Rather I am hoping that the course will change the way they view the world, that they will come to see the world as a morally active place and that they will begin to develop the skills to think and feel about the situations they have now been sensitized to.

This point is particularly important for students who are studying ethics as part of their professional development, as the object of their study will be of immediate and significant relevance to their professional lives. These medical students have to come to see moral concerns as being of concern to them, as affecting them, as being relevant to them. If they can do that, then the features of moral situations will 'stand out' more prominently for them. It may be that the very ability to perceive a situation as morally relevant is a skill we actually develop rather than one which is automatically and unproblematically shared by everyone, but its development is a crucial step in becoming morally aware. Hinnman draws an analogy between great art and moral wisdom. In the same way that great art reveals an entirely new way of viewing the world, it changes our perspective and provokes our emotional responses, moral wisdom also changes the way we view the world, sensitizing us to different aspects of the world, giving us a different viewpoint and engaging our emotions.[6]

2. Moral imagination

The first step in moral development then is to come to see the world differently, to come to see the world as a place full of situations that require our attention, our reflection and possibly our reaction. Mary Warnock writes on moral imagination:

> . . . there is a power in the human mind which is at work in our everyday perception of the world, and is also at work in our thoughts about what is absent; which enables us to see the world, whether present or absent as significant, and also to present this vision to others, for them to share or reject.[7]

In practical terms this may mean coming to see the world as others see it and coming to see ourselves in the world as playing particular roles shared by others in our professions or stations or roles in life. A doctor, for example, needs to come to see the world differently, with a certain degree of compassion and understanding for pain, suffering and vulnerability. This involves cultivating a particular sensitivity to situations concerning others who are in pain, who are suffering or who are in positions vulnerable to exploitation. This sensitivity is not merely a matter of complete identification with those others. A doctor who fully identified with all his patients would quickly become incapacitated through the emotional burden of all the pain and suffering around him. The correct approach lies in a mean, neither too little emotion, which makes a doctor cold, distant and ineffective in his attempts to connect with patients and appreciate their point of view, but neither too much emotion, which makes a doctor too involved and incapacitated by overwhelming emotions.

Students of morality also come to see the world as a morally alert place through the example of others. It is by seeing others react with concern, sympathy, anger, indignation, etc. that we come to realize that there may be cause for concern, sympathy, anger, indignation, etc. Students come to see certain aspects of the world as being of concern to them because they are of concern to those they wish to emulate. One of the most successful methods of getting students to see the importance of ethics to their chosen career is to include those who are already successful in this career as their teachers. If a practising doctor tells medical students that the study of ethics is not only useful but also indispensable to the practice of the profession they are more likely to take this advice on board. A practising doctor will also be able to come up with ethical examples that are directly relevant to the students' own future experiences, examples they can identify with and examples they can look out for when they observe practice. Similar points can be made for other professions or activities, for example, Sherman mentions how experienced naval officers play a significant role in the ethical education of midshipmen by providing relevant and accessible examples of ethical situations.[8] 'We learn best from those with whom we can identify and from those whom we value positively. This underlies Aristotle's view that friendship (*philia*) is the central arena in which character development takes place'.[9] Aristotelian friendship is based around a shared love of the good, so having the right friends in this respect is a crucial step in moral development. Friends and role models need not be perfect to be of use as friends and role models, but they do need to be oriented towards the good.

Similar remarks apply to teachers of ethics.[10] Probably as a result of teaching numerous classes on Aristotle and virtue ethics, I am sometimes asked by students if I am an example of the ideally virtuous agent (!). I chose to interpret this question in a flattering manner, and although the answer is invariably and emphatically 'no', it is worth remembering that teachers set the moral tone in classrooms. By this, I mean that teachers need to set the tone in terms of dignity, integrity and respect in a classroom. While intellectual sparing is at the heart of philosophical teaching and we expect our students (and ourselves) to ferociously attack the arguments of our opponents, this should never extend to personal attacks. It is the role of teachers to guide discussions away from the offensive and the personal and towards appropriate intellectual antagonism, instilling the virtues of both respect and integrity in intellectual debates in their students. It is the role of teachers to disapprove of disparaging remarks and make this disapproval known but without entirely destroying the confidence of the student who made the mistake – the point of mistakes is to learn from them, not to be annihilated by them.

> Decency and integrity in our everyday encounters are both important in themselves and likely to be important in strengthening our disposition to be moral when we face the big decisions. If we do not nurture ethics on the small scale, we may not get it on the grand scale either.[11]

How one behaves in everyday, relatively mundane encounters sets the tone for how one behaves when faced with more difficult and challenging moral problems. If one doesn't practice virtue in a small scale though, it is implausible to imagine that it will be effortlessly available to us in the grander scale. The teacher has to be genuinely enthusiastic, conscientious and engaged with morality if she has any chance of transmitting these attitudes and values to her students.

Relevant and accessible role models stimulate the students' moral imagination as does immersive role play and innovative methods of teaching, including the use of narrative, that encourage students to think for themselves. The importance of narrative cannot be underemphasized in this respect. Virtue ethicists often appeal to literary examples to make their points about moral character and this is because authors have a particular ability to present a fully immersive picture of the situations their characters come across. Novelists and playwrights specialize in bringing the background to the foreground, giving us an insight into the rich lives of their protagonists, in making us a part of the story they are telling. Such examples provide rich ground for discussion and employing similar techniques by asking students to take on 'personas' and act out scenarios engage the imagination.

It is also important that the teaching of ethics is fully integrated into teaching in general. Ethics is not a separate discipline, practised in a classroom and abandoned as soon as one exits the door. Teaching medical ethics to medical students alongside the teaching of anatomy, patient history, diagnostics, treatment, etc. mimics most closely the way these students will eventually come across ethical problems, that is as part of their professional practice, intertwined with clinical and socio-cultural aspects of the same case. The narratives mentioned earlier should include a richness of pathological, clinical, social and ethical elements to better represent what real patients are like.

In this section then, we have assumed a fairly wide role for moral imagination, both alerting us to moral situations, allowing us to contemplate alternative possibilities, helping us to immerse ourselves in the circumstances and aiding us to develop morally. I have hinted briefly at how moral imagination may be encouraged through relevant role models, appropriate teachers, detailed narratives and role play. All these techniques help us think about situations before we have to actually face them in real life, but thinking about morality is not enough, moral education crucially involves teaching in emotion.

3. The emotions revisited

According to the account of virtue ethics I have developed so far, it's not possible to think morally without feeling morally. We discussed the role of the emotions in Aristotelian character in Chapter 3; however, they play such an important role in character development that it is worth returning to the subject here. We can now identify a number of functions the emotions fulfil and relate them to moral education:

1 The world provokes emotions in us. It is the person's suffering that triggers our pity and our desire to help. How the world is can provoke different emotional reactions though. In some variations of the Good Samaritan experiments, the 'victims' were portrayed as dirty, off-putting and potential threatening. Unsurprisingly, seminary students were far less likely to help those 'victims' they perceived as potential threats than those they perceived as merely in need. By presenting the 'victim' as a potential threat the experimenters are alienating him and encouraging the subject to perceive him as outside the sphere of his moral obligations. In short, they are placing the subjects in a situation where it is difficult for them to empathize with the victim in the first place and where a great leap in perspectives is required for successfully taking into account the feelings and needs of the victim. The conditions of the experiment itself placed obstacles in the way of the proper exercise of empathic imagination, the proper exercise of which will have made it easier for the subjects to act morally. Instead of eliciting feelings of concern, sympathy and pity, the circumstances of the experiment were set up to elicit feelings of fear for one's well-being, and thus make emotional attachment and therefore kind action much more difficult. Milgram himself explains how some variations of his experiment were set up to make sure that '[t]he victim's suffering possesses an abstract, remote quality for the subject. He is aware, but only in a conceptual sense, that his actions cause pain to another person; the fact is apprehended but not felt'.[12] It should be no surprise that if we set people up to fail, they will fail.

The world not only provokes some emotions, but other emotions are impossible without reference to the world. For example, the emotion of shame only makes sense if the agent has carried out a dishonourable misdeed. If the agent judges his actions to have been justified and honourable, there is simply no room for shame.

What we should learn from these examples is the importance of setting people up to succeed, of appealing to what is best in them, of encouraging all naturally helpful tendencies and rewarding all positive emotions, of making it easy for them to empathize and to be emotionally moved in the right direction. The emotions make it possible for us to understand others, empathize with their predicaments so it makes a huge difference what kind of people and situations we come across, how we perceive them and what kinds of emotional reactions they generate in us. Learning from the experiments in personality psychology, we know that moral development must be a managed process. Students must be exposed to easy tests to promote learning and growth, before they face greater challenges.

> The social-psychological research points to the same conclusion: If we bend so easily before the winds of situational pressures, then we need opportunities during development, if not to face the strongest winds, as [sic] least to deal with some of the complexities and pressures of real situations.[13]

2   A kind person will be moved to feel sympathy and concern for someone in need but will also view that person as someone in need because of his feelings of sympathy and concern. Our emotional responses colour how we construe and understand situations. The right emotions allow us to perceive the world in a particular way, they move us by bringing particular features of situations to our attention and the very same thing can be perceived differently due to our emotional filters. For example, an arm extended in an attempt to touch someone may be perceived as a threat if the touching is judged to be unwelcome and fearful or as an

act of love if the touching is perceived to be supportive and welcome.

Appropriate emotions allow as to interpret situations correctly, for example, as requiring a response of kindness, or indignation or shame. Aristotle writes, 'The emotions are all those affections which cause men to change their opinion in regard to their judgements. . .',[14] and modern author, Nancy Sherman, elaborates:

> We can think of them [emotions] as modes of attention enabling us to notice what is morally salient, important, or urgent in ourselves and our surroundings. They help us track the morally relevant 'news'. They are a medium by which we discern the particulars. . .Moreover, emotions draw us in in a way that grabs hold of our attention and puts to the top of our priority orderings, thoughts or actions regarding these matters. We focus with intensity and impact, making inferences that might otherwise not have arisen or been thought of in as compelling a way.[15]

The emotions allow us to perceive the world in a particular way, so it is important that we cultivate the right emotions in the first place. A teacher who has been encouraged to feel that students are a distraction from his real job of doing research will become impatient and unwilling to listen to his students. This in turn will make their demands, questions and problems appear trivial, annoying and insignificant. The teacher's feelings of irritation and boredom will cloud how he perceives teaching and its demands, in a sense making teaching irritating and boring. Teachers should try to cultivate feelings of patience, understanding and care towards their students, so that they come to see their students in patient, understanding and caring ways.

3   Crucially the emotions motivate us to act. As we saw in Chapter 4 Section B, simply doing the right thing is not enough; the right act must be accompanied by the right emotion. Our example in that chapter, John, the young man who saves the drowning child to impress his girlfriend, has a rich emotional involvement in what he is doing, it just

isn't the right one! He may well be feeling pride, concern for himself, possibly even love for Anne, the girlfriend, but none of these emotions are relevant here. They motivate him to act, and coincidentally his act coincides with the right act in this situation, but overall what he has done has not proceeded from the right character trait. The desire to save the drowning child should be motivated by feelings of concern for the life about to be lost, not feelings of concern for one's self and how one appears to those one wants to impress. Self-centred emotions are inappropriate here and although they have, coincidentally, led to the right action in this situation, there is little reason to think they will do so again in the future.

The person who is appropriately concerned with the welfare of others can rely on these emotions to motivate him on multiple occasions when the welfare of others is concerned. The person who is inappropriately concerned with his own welfare will look after the welfare of others only when it happens to coincide with his concerns. Having the right emotions commit us to the right actions because we have the right concerns and come to view the world in the right way.

Even difficult acts can be made better by displaying the right emotion. Doctors cannot always treat patients and will sometimes have to turn patients down for reasons not directly related to their welfare. A doctor who has to tell a patient that there aren't sufficient funds for his medical treatment can do so with compassion, patience, understanding and support or can do so with disregard, impatience, cruelty and boredom. The result is the same, the patient does not get treated for financial reasons and this is a terrible outcome, but if the outcome cannot be avoided, the way it is explained to the patient makes all the difference.

4   Finally, the emotions convey our values to others, they let them know what we care about, what moves us, what upsets us. The account of the emotions I have relied upon in this chapter sees them not as blind, random and uncontrollable feelings but as part of our moral judgements. Aristotle characterizes the emotions as produced by evaluations. Circumstances excite and account for the emotions, for example, the sick man is easily provoked

with respect to his illness because this is what makes
him vulnerable; the lover is easily provoked with respect
to his love-affairs because this is what he cares about.
Our relationships with others account for and shape our
emotions, for example, we are more angry with our friends
if they let us down than with total strangers, because relying
on our friends is part of friendship. Our emotions display
to others what we think and care about, for example,
anger would not be anger without a judgement that one
had been unjustly treated, fear would not be fear without
the judgement that one was under threat.[16] In this sense,
our emotional commitments display that we have taken
responsibility for our actions, that our actions are the
product of who we are and an expression of our agency.

The emotions then play a crucial role in moral education and
it matters greatly what one feels, towards whom and in what
circumstances. We should habituate ourselves in the right responses
towards pleasure and pain in the hopes, that over time, what is
habit becomes second nature.

4. Change

The final aspect of moral education I would like to discuss is the
idea of change, development, progress, growth but also failure,
disappointment and regression. Moral development is not a period
restricted to childhood, but an ongoing process that takes up the
whole of one's life. Gradual self-understanding is crucial to this
process and that requires both learning from successes but also
adapting in response to failures. It is the responses to failure that
provide some of the most interesting insights in the personality
psychology experiments.

Milgram discusses a number of different reactions from subjects
who had surprised even themselves by following the immoral
dictates of authority, including:

A subject who wrote to the experimenters seeking a career
change, from engineering he wanted to change to psychology as
this subject is "much more important in today's world".[17]

Morris Braveman, a subject who reported: "What appalled me was that I could possess this capacity for obedience and compliance to a central idea, i.e. the value of a memory experiment even after it became clear that continued adherence to this value was at the expense of violation of another value, i.e. don't hurt someone else who is helpless and not hurting you. As my wife said, 'You can call yourself Eichmann'. I hope I can deal more effectively with any future conflicts of values I encounter"[18].

another subject who reported: "To me, the experiment pointed up...the extent to which each individual should have or discover firm ground on which to base his decision, no matter how trivial they appear to be. I think people should think more deeply about themselves and their relation to their world and other people. If this experiment serves to jar people out of complacency, it will have served its end"[19].

The number of people who obeyed authority in the Milgram experiments may have been a surprise, but what is a far more interesting reaction to consider is the response of these subjects to their own failure. The first subject in the quote above made a complete change in his life as a result of the experiments. The way he had behaved led him to re-examine what was important in his life and what he should be devoting his professional life to. This is a radical rethinking of what the good life consists in for this man, a fundamental change of direction in terms of what he finds important, what he wants to direct his efforts and attention to. The second subject above, Morris Bravemen, was led to reflect on his own actions. By his own admission, he was appalled by what he had done and was also led to reconsidering his reasoning process and how he made judgements about values. Being aware of his mistake and the ways in which he erred is bound to help him avoid the same errors in the future. Finally, the third subject is led to a radical reconsideration of the importance of morality. What he had thought was a trivial, unimportant, simple decision, revealed itself in retrospect to have been of significant importance, affecting the man's relationship to others and the world in general. Here is an example of someone who, through a very sharp awakening, has become more sensitive to the moral complexities of the world.

We hope for incremental improvement in our moral development, but we have to be prepared to learn from the inevitable, but hopefully only occasional failures. When these failures do occur, their lessons have the potential of being deeply felt and meaningful as they reveal our weaknesses and the areas of our own character that should most concern us and attract our attention for improvement in the future. The biggest lessons in moral education come from ourselves, and while we should take justified pride in our successes, it is our failures that we learn most from. The examples above reveal that people are willing to learn from their failures and will, as a result, take even drastic steps to change their lives. Failure is an integral part of moral education, especially when it can be stage-managed so that it is instructive rather than destructive. The role of moral education with respect to failure is to allow it to take place in a controlled manner so that it can lead to lessons learnt and not annihilation.

Failure is also one of the many things we can learn from by observing others. We do not need perfect role models, as there is a lot we can learn from imperfect ones. Observing the failures of others can give us warning about our own pitfalls as long, of course, as we are aware that what we are observing is a mistake and not an example to emulate.

This chapter has an impossibly ambitious goal in attempting to give an account of moral education in the virtues. However, it has been worth grappling with, nonetheless. Partly because this chapter attempts to give the beginnings of answers to questions that arise naturally from the position we have considered in this volume. If our main aim is to learn how to think and feel morally, then virtue ethics owes us some account of how this is possible, how we become sensitized to the world, how we develop moral perception and how we build on moral wisdom. Partly because the chapters in this section are springboards for further discussion and ideas about what might lie in the future for research in virtue ethics. And partly because the main questions virtue ethics asks, 'What kind of person should I be? How should I live my life?', are practical questions that require practical answers.

This chapter has rejected some of the distinctions that shape discourse in modern discussions of moral education. It has rejected the choice between two rival versions of moral education, one whose focus is on mindless development of character through unreflective habits and the other whose focus is on reasoning skills concerned with applying principles. Neither option is satisfactory. We learn through example, through habit, through repetition, but the aim is to develop understanding, to internalize the relevant values and chose virtue for its own sake. The basis of moral authority is the right reason, which we are able to perceive through our natural ability to reason and feel, but the process of developing moral wisdom is tough and gradual, requires personal development, discovery and sensitization in both reason and emotion, rather than indoctrination or direct instruction. The road to virtue is not only shaped by situational factors which go towards making us who we are but is also entirely vulnerable to them. One role of moral education is to manage these situational factors, expose us to the best influences, test us only when appropriate and to a degree which we can reasonably hope to learn from rather than be devastated by. Finally, moral education cannot teach us what to do, it has to content with trying to teach us how to think and how to feel; what we do with these abilities, what kinds of characters we develop and what kinds of actions these characters result in, is up to us.

Further readings

Lickona also argues that the personality psychology experiments are useful for gaining insights on how we should teach ethics using arguments which parallel the ones in this chapter, Lickona, in Callahan, and Bok, 1980. For an overview of the history of character and moral education, see Arthur, in Nucci and Narvaez, 2008.

For more on moral imagination and its place in Aristotelian character development, see Hartman, 2000, Kekes, 1991, and Pardales, 2002. On the central role of narrative in character development, see MacIntyre, 1981.

Aristotle's views on the emotions are developed in the *Art of Rhetoric*. An excellent modern account of Aristotle on the emotions and character development can be found in Sherman, 1989, while the collection by Carr and Steutel is well worth taking a look at for more in-depth accounts of virtue ethics and moral education, Carr and Steutel, 1999, or for an overview of Aristotle on moral education, see Carr, in Nucci and Narvaez, 2008. If you have a particular interest in the education of medical students and other professionals, you might want to read Athanassoulis, in Ashcroft et al., 2007.

CHAPTER NINE

The Kantian response

1. The role of the categorical imperative

We started off this volume by examining how virtue ethics emerged out of a sense of dissatisfaction with the other two alternative moral theories, deontology and consequentialism. This critique of the two rivals rested on a particular conception of these theories and a specific understanding of their claims which was then used to draw attention to the weaknesses and deficiencies of the theories which would be remedied by virtue ethics. Within this context it is understandable that the increase in interest in virtue ethics was accompanied by responses to its criticisms from the rival camps. The responses concentrated on two areas: first, they deny the understanding of deontology that virtue ethicists rely on to build their critique and, second, they show how the purported advantages of virtue ethics are also shared by deontology. In a sense then the picture painted in Part I of this volume is unrepresentative, not because it is incorrect but rather because it is incomplete. To fully understand virtue ethics, we need to come full circle and examine the kinds of responses that the virtue ethical critique has provoked. While consequentialists have been equally vigorous in the defence of their theories as deontologists, practical constraints limit us to examining just one of the theories, so for our purposes we will only examine the Kantian response to virtue ethics.

In responding to the virtue ethical challenge, modern deontologists have shifted their focus to lesser researched works by Kant such as the *Metaphysics of Morals*, the *Religion within the Boundaries of Mere Reason* and the *Anthropology from a Pragmatic Point of View*. These works show a different aspect of Kant's work, one which might lead us to revise how we should interpret his overall theory. Modern deontologists have, in the same way that virtue ethicists have reinterpreted Aristotelian ideas, often gone beyond Kant's own works, to consider expanded and altered accounts of his theory. In this chapter, we will try to follow some of the main discussions in this area, in particular those that correspond to the themes discussed in Part I of this volume.

One of the most serious objections raised by virtue ethicists against deontologists is that they rely on rigid, inflexible rules that do not capture the particular details of situations and therefore do not account for the diversity of ethical life. A promising response to this objection is to re-conceive the role of the Categorical Imperative. The aim of the *Groundwork of the Metaphysics of Morals* is to search for the supreme principle of morality, but this doesn't mean that this supreme principle will give us an *easy* answer to all moral problems or that *all* answers to moral problems can be given by sole reference to this principle. In this sense, the term 'principle' is misleading here if we understand by it an overriding rule which operates as a concrete guide to action. Rather than a concrete guide to actions, the supreme principle of morality is conceived as a Categorical Imperative because it guides action from an inner moral constraint. Acting from duty is acting from an inner acknowledgement of the binding force of morality on us as a constraint and as a command. When we act from duty, we are motivated by the 'purely rational appeal of a universally valid rational principle'[1] rather than being motivated by our inclinations and empirical natures. To understand this, we need to make a small detour and consider Kant's views on our empirical nature.

As we shall see in the third section of this chapter, Kant does make room in his account of morality for our desires and inclinations, but their role differs fundamentally from that of desires in Aristotelian theory. This is because Kant has a different starting point with respect to his views on desires, inclinations and the empirical side of human nature. Kant deeply mistrusts our inclinations; he views humans as likely to be blinded by self-deceit because of inclinations that mislead us and distort the demands of morality. For example, because we are (naturally) full of self-conceit we misjudge ourselves to be morally better than we are; because we are (naturally) full of jealousy we misjudge others to be morally worse than they are. Humans have a propensity to evil, so we must constantly guard against the motive of self-love and we must always view our natural inclinations with mistrust. The source of moral worth, therefore, can never be inclinations as they are both likely to mislead us and be fickle, unreliable and not under our control. The supreme principle of morality cannot be derived from empirical considerations and our grounds for acting cannot be inclination.

This doesn't mean that inclinations have no value, just that they have no *moral value*, as we shall see later on in this chapter. Nor does it mean that our empirical natures have no place in Kantian theory, rather that they have a very specific place. Our empirical natures cannot be the grounds of our actions, our actions must be constrained by our rational natures as instantiated in the Categorical imperative, but the very point of some of Kant's later works such as the *Metaphysics of Morals* is to show how the application of the supreme principle of morality is constrained by our empirical natures and situated in the empirical world. The Categorical Imperative is a test for maxims and there are two broad responses to how maxims should be understood as 'subjective principles of action'[2]: either the *formulation* of maxims admits of qualifications and/or the *application* of maxims admits of sensitivity to particulars. To act from duty is to follow a Categorical Imperative even against all inclinations, so the *grounds* of our actions cannot be found in our empirical natures, but that doesn't mean that the *formulation* of our maxims and/or the *application* of our actions cannot reflect our empirical natures.

Onora O'Neill's account of maxims is an example of how the formulation of maxims admits of qualifications. For O'Neill, the role of the maxim is to capture features of the act on which the agent's choice depends, so the formulation of the maxim is already discriminatory. That is, not just any formulation will do, but rather only the formulation that captures the agent's intentions: 'For what will be decisive is what an agent's fundamental intention or principle in doing a given act really is. What counts is whether the expression of falsehood expresses a fundamental attempt to deceive, or whether agreement with another (in itself innocent enough) expresses a fundamental refusal to judge or think for oneself'.[3] An agent can't get away with universalizing a very narrow maxim to deceive such as 'I will lie only when I can get away with it and it benefits myself', because the intention expressed in the maxim, that is, to deceive, is not universalizable. This approach generates maxims sensitive to the particulars of situations, thus satisfying the concerns of the virtue ethicist, while maintaining the core ideas of Kantian thought, namely that the theory should be grounded in notions of rationality and pure moral worth rather than empirical considerations.[4]

The other possible avenue is to argue that the application of the maxims allows for context and sensitivity to our empirical nature, and therefore requires judgement. Barbara Herman reconceives of maxims as 'deliberative presumptions'. The Categorical Imperative does not give us rules for action but is a test for very generic maxims of the type 'Do X for Y reason'. When a generic maxim fails the test of the Categorical Imperative, it generates a deliberative presumption against doing actions of that type for reasons of that kind. Reminiscent of *prima facie* duties, deliberative presumptions are defeasible moral considerations that serve as general rules against exemptions from self-interest and can be defeated only if in specific circumstances the agent's actual maxim is not one of self-interest. The defeasibility of deliberative presumptions therefore requires contextual judgement. Herman's approach allows for a great deal of context sensitivity, although some may worry that this comes at the cost of moving too far from Kant's original ideas.

Finally, some neo-Kantians see both the formulation and the application of maxims as related to empirical context. For example, Allen Wood argues that, for Kant, practical judgement is the capacity to move from a universal principle to practical instances of it, but that capacity cannot be substituted by more principles, rather it is a capacity acquired by experience and practice.[5] While the authority of the Categorical Imperative is independent of our empirical nature, the rules that derive from it must be interpreted in light of empirical facts about human beings and their application takes place in a particular context, none of which can be captured in rigid rules.[6] Wood concludes: 'The point is that when it comes to applying moral rules or duties, what moral agents need is not to be *told what to do*, but rather they need guidance in *thinking for themselves* about what they choose to do'.[7] These final thoughts about the role of moral judgement are very much in accord with what a virtue ethicist might have to say on the topic, although it is interesting to note that if there is any force to the objection that virtue ethics is not action guiding because it is not sufficiently prescriptive, the very same objection now applies to Kantians.

Another way in which the interpretation of the role of Categorical Imperative can resist the virtue ethical objection of inflexibility is to focus on imperfect duties, an idea we will examine in the next section.

2. Imperfect duties and impartiality

Kant distinguishes between two kinds of duties, perfect and imperfect duties. Perfect duties like 'Do not lie (from the motive of self-interest and with the intention to deceive)' are negative duties prohibiting actions from certain motives. It is these duties that the Categorical Imperative is meant to be a test for. If a maxim fails the test of the Categorical Imperative, then there is a perfect duty to not act in this way and this duty cannot be overridden by inclinations. Imperfect duties, however, are different. Rather than forbidding an action done from a particular motive, they command the pursuit of an end. For example, we have imperfect duties towards ourselves to develop our talents and imperfect duties towards others to promote their happiness. While both perfect and imperfect duties are similar in the sense that they command with the same force, they differ in that imperfect duties allow us quite a bit of latitude in how we realize the end they command. There are a variety of actions that qualify as promoting the happiness of others, and imperfect duties allow us room to decide when, how and towards whom we fulfil the duty.

Because of this interpretation of imperfect duties, neo-Kantians need not be tied down to inflexible, prescriptive and limited rules, but can take account of the variety of the circumstances of the moral life. There are many different ways of promoting other people's happiness and Kant's thoughts are perfectly compatible with allowing room for the agent to interpret how and when this is done. This interpretation of Kant on imperfect duties has a number of implications. According to Marcia Baron, it allows for a number of conceptions of the good life. It allows the Kantian to recognize the diversity of natural talents people may have and allow them to develop in different ways. Furthermore, a person may fulfil her imperfect duties through developing her artistic talents and spending some of her time on charitable causes without having to become an entirely self-sacrificing altruist in the cause of promoting the happiness of others. The moral saint is not the Kantian ideal and indeed being a moral saint may be problematic under the Kantian understanding of morality as it involves a very one-sided preoccupation with the happiness of others which may well involve a corresponding neglect of one's own talents. Baron quotes Kant in support of this interpretation of the rejection of the life of the moral saint, who seems to suggest, in the *Critique of Practical Reason*, that the man who gives his life to save others will have done a good thing in accordance with duty, but in losing his life will have infringed on his duties to himself (once dead he can no longer fulfil any of his talents).[8]

Another implication of the existence of imperfect duties is that having an imperfect duty to promote the happiness of others is perfectly compatible with aiding some people more than others, so would allow for special treatment of those who are near and dear to us. The virtue ethical objection that other theories fail to account for partial relationships like family ties and friendships may have more force against theories that require the maximization of impersonal value than Kantianism. So, for example, Utilitarianism requires moral agents to maximize utility with no reference as to whose utility is being maximized, all 'units' of utility count equally with no regard for who they benefit. As a result, Utilitarianism is far more vulnerable to the objection that it cannot account for the special status of friendships. However, Kantianism is not a theory requiring us to promote impersonal value. Baron argues that it is perfectly permissible to show preferential treatment to other people some of the time. Preferential treatment is only problematic when it shows a morally unjustifiable preference.[9] To make sense of this conclusion, we need to reconsider what is impartiality and why there might be a requirement for impartiality.

Aristotle enjoins us to '[t]reat equals equally and unequals unequally'.[10] The advice at first seems a bit vacuous as it seems self-evident, but the point of the claim is that the difficult task in just distributions is to determine who is equal to whom and according to what standard of equality. In Chapter 2, Section B, we saw how this applied to philosophy essays, essays that showed equally good elements of a good philosophy essay were warranted the same mark, but at the centre of this understanding of just distributions of marks was the conception of what counts as a good essay. Neo-Kantians argue that their theory can accommodate the same insights.

Consider Baron's example about what kind of partial treatment you are allowed to give: it is permissible to invite some people over to dinner on the grounds that you like them and not invite others on the grounds that you do not like them as much, but it is not permissible to only offer your help to those who desperately need it because you like them and ignore those you do not like.[11] This is because people in general do not have a claim to becoming your dinner guests, but they do have a claim to your aid when they desperately need it. There is room for choice in deciding who you invite to dinner and there is room for favouring those you like; however, the same is not true with respect to emergency, life-saving aid. Aristotle would have no quarrel with any of this, as the legitimacy of partial considerations can only be justified within certain contexts that allow latitude for partial choices. 'That he is my friend' is an acceptable justification of some partial choices, for example, why I give him my time and emotional support as opposed to a stranger, but not others, for example, why I gave him the job over a more qualified candidate.

If impartiality then is defined as not treating others unfairly but definitionally allows for differential treatment and allows for special consideration where such consideration is *warranted*, then both Aristotelian and Kantian theories are impartial in this sense and can both account for the importance of friendships and other relationships in our lives, as well as allowing space for these relationships within our understanding of morality.[12] The virtue ethical objection then that Kantians do not allow room in their theory for relationships that are fundamental to living the good life no longer seems as relevant.

The reinterpretation of the Categorical Imperative, the refocusing of attention on imperfect duties and the re-examination of the requirements of impartiality allow neo-Kantians to offer convincing responses to the virtue ethical objection about the problems associated with rigid rules. In the next section, we will examine the degree of similarity between the Aristotelian and Kantian views on the emotions.

3. Acting from duty and the emotions

It seems incontrovertible that there are some passages in Kant's works that suggest that he had a deep mistrust of the emotions and argued if not for expunging them at least for not allowing them any role in the moral sphere. For example, the long passage we considered in Chapter 3, Section A, on the distinction between the 'friend of man' who acts out of inclination and whose act therefore has no moral worth and the man who acts out of duty and therefore has true moral worth. Kant's mistrust of the emotions arises from a variety of sources. Kant is concerned that the emotions are unreliable. Their source is our natural temperament or the circumstances that provoke them, neither of which are under our control. Emotions may be present at some times but not at others, they may appear in response to some circumstances but not others, so again we do not have power over them. Moral emotions cannot be called upon at will when they are needed and therefore cannot be the proper subject of moral praise and blame as we are not responsible for having or not having them. Also, many of our inclinations originate from what Kant sees as suspect sources. As human beings, it is our natural pathology to be overwhelmed by our desires. The motive of self-love is the motive we must guard against the most as this motive makes subjective considerations about our own well-being and self-interest into the objective determinant of the will.[13] Essentially what this means is that we are prone to taking on our desires as overriding moral considerations and therefore all our desires are suspect as grounds for morality because they tend to place us over others and give our empirical concerns priority over the demands of morality. Emotions cannot be the foundation of morality as they are not objective. Finally, the emotions are only, at best, incidentally aligned to the good. For example, sympathy may incline us to help someone who is doing evil because the emotions cannot distinguish between evil and good.

Neo-Kantians have developed two lines of thought in response to this, admittedly, problematic approach to the emotions. I say 'problematic' because, on the whole, modern thinkers have accepted that there ought to be a greater role for the emotions than that assigned to them by the ideas presented above. While it is possible to 'bite the bullet' and simply concur with Kant that he was right to mistrust the emotions, on the whole, the responses in the literature tend to accept that a plausible account of morality needs to allow a greater role for the emotions than that suggested by the passages above (or at least by the passages above examined in isolation). The two lines of thought then, which are not mutually exclusive, are first to highlight the kinds of emotions Kant does allow room for and second to elaborate on the ways emotions can play different roles in Kantian theory. The latter strategy is more of a matter of interpretation and development of Kant's ideas and so results in a number of different approaches. We will return to this thought shortly; first, we will consider the kinds of emotions Kant does allow room for.

Acting from the motive of duty has some affective aspects because it gives rise to a particular kind of emotion, a feeling of respect for the moral law. We all have certain feelings by virtue of being human which lie at the basis of morality and make us receptive to the demands of duty, that is, we are naturally predisposed to be affected by moral considerations. These feelings are moral feeling, conscience, love of one's neighbour and respect for oneself[14] and they are all related to the moral law. Moral feeling is the sense of pleasure or displeasure that comes from acting from duty or failing to do so. Conscience is not something we acquire but a fact of our being that we are aligned with morality. Love of others and respect for oneself are based on the recognition that we and other humans are capable of being constrained by the moral law. These feelings are all aroused by our consciousness of the moral law, and similarly there are negative feelings of guilt, shame and contempt towards ourselves and others when we fail to do our duty.[15]

Allen Wood also interprets Kant as allowing room for rational desires that accompany reason. These rational desires may at first glance seem similar to trained Aristotelian desires that go hand in hand with the right reason, but a closer look reveals quite a different account of the role of rational desires. In Aristotle, appropriate desires help us notice the requirement for action, help us determine what we should do and motivate us to do the right thing. In Kant, reason reveals our obligations and then also produces a feeling of pleasure, a special emotion of reverence for the moral law accompanied by joy at our willing what reason requires of us. Desires have no place as grounds for our motivation, even if they happen to be the right kinds of desires, but desires are produced by our pursuit of the objects of our rational choice.[16] The ordering of the desires here is entirely different; for Aristotle, rational desires reveal morally salient particulars and are part of practical judgement; for Kant, rational desires are a by-product of the work done by reason alone.

While there is ample evidence of these special moral emotions in Kant's writing, there is a worry that appeal to them doesn't do much for promoting a plausible account of our actual experience as emotional beings. These moral feelings are, if anything, rather peculiar instances of emotional sensitivity and there are concerns that in places Kant's appeal to them becomes almost mystical and akin to religious fervour – none of which helps with responding to the objection that the Kantian picture fails to take into account the important role of human emotions.

The second line of thought open to neo-Kantians is to find more substantial roles for emotions, a task which overwhelmingly requires reinterpreting if not reconstructing Kant's own views. Marcia Baron asks us to reconsider our reading of Kant's rejection of the inclinations as presented in the quote above. She argues that this particular passage is purposefully exaggerated in order to highlight the importance of acting from duty. She also argues that the contrast Kant is concerned with here is not one between two people, one of whom lacks inclination but possesses duty, and the other possessing inclination but lacking duty; rather, the correct contrast is between two people, both of whom have the right inclinations but only one of whom has a conception of the demands of duty.[17] However, this response moves quite far away from some of the fundamental Kantian claims. It allows some value to be placed on having the right inclinations, but seems to suggest that acting from the motive of duty then carries the day. It seems to make the motive of duty an extra point in favour of the agent's motivation, whereas it should be the only ground for determining the agent's moral worth and as such it may not be a solution acceptable to all Kantians.

Perhaps one way out of this problem is to consider the contrast between acting from inclination which has no moral worth and acting from duty *with* inclination, which has moral worth and allows a role for the emotions. What exactly could this role be? Margaret Baxley suggests that we should reject inclinations as the ground of action because they are opposed to morality, but that we can allow room for inclinations that have been cultivated in accordance with reason. The *Metaphysics of Morals* gives numerous examples of calls to cultivate those feelings which are responsive to the power of reason and play a variety of roles such as facilitating the choices involved in specifying imperfect duties, prompting beneficent actions and allowing us to fulfil the requirements of reason in a humane way.[18] The success of such approaches will depend on how much room can be afforded to the emotions without making them the determining ground of the will. To further understand the possibilities here, we need to examine the Kantian understanding of virtue.

4. Virtue as strength of will

To understand Kant's account of virtue, we need to appeal to a distinction which is central in Kant's thought: the distinction between the intelligible (noumenal) and the sensible (phenomenal) worlds. A word of warning is appropriate before we move on; this is an extremely complex distinction, with a multiplicity of layers and implications for Kantian thought, and we can only give it the most cursory examination. The following discussion should be read with this caution in mind.

We are part of two worlds. The sensible world is the world of appearances, subject to causal laws that are naturally necessitated, and therefore it is difficult to see how freedom and choice are possible in this world. However, as moral agents we are also part of the intelligible world, transcendentally free and therefore can be held responsible for our choices. The intelligible world is the world of things-in-themselves, understood through reason alone, a capacity available to all human beings, at all times and with no reference to their background or prior circumstances. The intelligible world allows for an *a priori* conception of the fundamental principle of morality which owes nothing to empirical contingencies, while the empirical world allows for a plausible picture of human nature as subject to empirical contingencies – the challenge is how to reconcile these two worlds.

Correspondingly, Kant has two conceptions of virtue, virtue in the intelligible world and virtue in the sensible world. Virtue in the intelligible world is a conception of moral character (*Denkungsart*), a reorientation of the will towards the good, a sudden revolution of the will from the principle of self-love to the principle of duty. It is a commitment to morality that is available to everyone, any time, regardless of their background and empirical considerations. This change of heart to a commitment to the moral duty is the mark of real moral worth and cannot be brought about through any empirical influences such as habits or education.

Virtue is present in the sensible world as well, as a disposition of strength of temperament in resisting inclinations (*Sinnesart*). Sensible virtue involves a change of mores, a gradual change of the empirical character that can be brought about through the development of right habits, education and other empirical influences.

Virtue involves struggle in both conceptions. In the intelligible conception, there is struggle as we are only finitely rational beings and feel the commands of morality as constraints. If the perception of the force of morality were absent, we would have holly wills, but we do not, so we feel constrained by the moral 'ought'. At the same time, virtue is a struggle in the empirical world as we are led astray by our inclinations and virtue is the struggle to resist contrary inclinations.[19] However, struggle and a negative conception are not the only aspects of virtue. Virtue in the intelligible world is also self-constraint in accordance with the principle of inner freedom, so virtue is its own reward[20] and this recognition of the moral law produces, as we saw above, positive feelings of satisfaction and joy.[21] In turn though, because we are also beings in the sensible world, we can experience the feeling of reverence for the moral law reluctantly and feel humiliated by having to pay tribute to the merit of others.[22]

The above is a very brief summary of some very complex ideas, but I want us to take two things from this discussion. The first is that any comparison between Aristotelian virtue and Kantian virtue is unlikely to be straightforward. The second is that a major challenge for neo-Kantians is to reconcile the account of the intelligible world with the account of the sensible world.

It should be evident from the discussions so far that both Aristotle and Kant have rich conceptions of virtue, which relate to many other ideas within their theories and that therefore any comparison of the concepts could never be a quick and simple affair. Kant's account of empirical virtue certainly seems to have many points of similarity to Aristotelian virtue and therefore can be used by Kantians in response to the virtue ethical objections. Aristotle and Kant agree that although virtue is not habit in itself, habit is a useful tool for virtue. Unreflective repetition, though, which is how habitual action should be understood, cannot be true virtue as virtue involves choice.[23] However, Aristotle and Kant disagree on the precise role habit plays. For Aristotle, unreflective habit is a starting point, habituating oneself in 'the that' will eventually, along with other developments, lead to understanding 'the because'. For Kant, the starting point is acceptance of the moral law, habituation may help shape practices, but virtue requires a conversion in one's perspective, a reorientation towards the good (a revolution in the *Denkungsart*) which is not linked to one's habits.

Character development therefore has a similar profile in both theories, that is, it plays an important role, it is gradual and subject to external influences, but the place of character development differs in the two theories. Primary in the Kantian picture is the exercise of reason which is the affirmation of the force of the moral law. While for Aristotle it is also central to choose virtue, do so knowingly and for its own sake, this choice is only possible through the development of the empirical character and may be impossible if thwarted by unfortunate empirical circumstances. For Kant empirical considerations are at best a temporary substitute for reason and this is most evident in his account of the role of emotions.

For Aristotle, the emotions play a significant and central role in the development of virtue and are seen primarily as a positive influence, at least as long as they are under the sway of positive influences and able to be shaped by reason. For Kant, the emotions are primarily suspect as contrary influences and their role is merely supplemental or temporary until reason can take over:

> The principle of *apathy* – namely that the wise man must never be in a state of affect, not even in that of compassion with the misfortune of his best friend, is an entirely correct and sublime moral principle of the Stoic school; for affect makes us (more or less) blind. – Nevertheless, the wisdom of nature has planted in us the predisposition to compassion in order to handle the reins *provisionally*, until reason has achieved the necessary strength; that is to say, for the purpose of enlivening us, nature has added the incentive of pathological (sensible) impulse to the moral incentives of the good, as a temporary surrogate of reason.[24]

While Aristotelian virtue is a state of balance between the right reason and the right desire, both necessary for and leading to the right action, Kantian virtue is a state of struggle against contrary inclinations and involves a feeling of resentment towards the commanding force of morality. Some commentators have suggested that this is a problem for Kant, as Kantian virtue is therefore 'merely' continence, but I think that this objection fails to see that this is not a like-for-like comparison. Kantian virtue is not comparable to Aristotelian continence as it isn't supported by the same account of the relationship between reason and the emotions. Kantian virtue is not a *lesser* account of virtue than Aristotle's account of virtue because it is fundamentally about struggle; it is a *different* account. It is only within the Aristotelian scheme that we have progression from struggle – continence and incontinence – to stability – virtue; in the Kantian scheme, inclinations always remain suspect, so struggle against them is the only possible state for being such as us.

Aristotle and Kant have similar things to say about the role of the virtuous person. Neither is interest in the virtuous person as a direct example, as neither holds much stock in the possibility of achieving virtue by directly copying the actions of another. As we have seen, the Aristotelian emphasis is on the *orthos logos* and the virtuous person's abilities to perceive it and act in accordance with it. Kant's interest in the virtuous person is similar:

> The *experimental* (technical) means for cultivating virtue is *good* example on the part of the teacher (his exemplary conduct) and *cautionary* example in others, since, for a still undeveloped human being, imitation is the first determination of his will to accept maxims that he afterwards makes for himself. – To form a habit is to establish a lasting inclination apart from any maxim, through frequently repeated gratifications of that inclination; it is a mechanism of sense rather than a principle of thought (and one that is easier to *acquire* that *to get rid of* afterwards). – As for the power of examples (good or bad) that can be held up to the propensity for imitation or warning, what others give us can establish no maxim of virtue. For, a maxim of virtue consists precisely in the subjective autonomy of each human being's practical reason and so implies that the law itself, not the conduct of other human beings, must serve as our incentive . . . A good example (exemplary conduct) should not serve as a model but only as a proof that it is really possible to act in conformity with duty. So it is not comparison with any other human being whatsoever (as he is), but with the *idea* (of humanity), as he ought to be, and so comparison with the law, that must serve as the constant standard of a teacher's instruction.[25]

Finally, while reason plays a central role in Aristotelian theory, and there are convincing comparisons between the importance of the concept of the noble and the good in Aristotle and the importance of the moral law in Kant,[26] the Kantian emphasis on the intelligible world and in general Kantian metaphysics do not have a direct comparison with Aristotle's work. If one had to compare the relative merits of the two theories in one sentence, I think that one would say that the greatest challenge for Aristotle is providing an account of the objective grounding of virtue, while the greatest challenge for Kant is reconciling the relationship between the empirical and the intelligible worlds.

The task for neo-Kantians is to demonstrate the continuity and the overall coherence of the Kantian project, from metaphysics to moral psychology, from the intelligible to the empirical, from his earlier works to his later works. Kant does have convincing, plausible answers to the virtue ethical objections; his theory has the resources to account of the complexity of moral practice, to accommodate friendship and other partial relationships, to permit a role for the emotions, to find room for virtue and character. The answers Kantians give are not identical to the Aristotelian approach, there are significant similarities but also significant differences between the two theories, but they are interesting answers nonetheless that reveal a rich conception of morality. The question that still requires work is how all these ideas cohere with Kant's metaphysical claims.

Further readings

Most of the suggestions for further readings relevant to this chapter are available in the footnotes. However, more specifically, for anyone interested in direct comparisons of Aristotle and Kant on virtue and character, Sherman, 1997, is an excellent, detailed and insightful account; Baron et al., 1997, is a very good introduction and more resources can be found in Beltzer, 2008 and Athanassoulis, 2005.

Conclusion for
Part Three

In this part of the book we have considered three different, but interrelated topics, brought together under the heading of 'current developments' in virtue ethics. The inclusion of these chapters in the present volume is significant because it gives some indication of further areas of research in this exciting field and may even prompt some readers to take up these topics for themselves. The disadvantage of this approach of attempting to cover three large areas of debate in three short chapters is that at our conclusion some crucial questions still remain unanswered. Readers interested in pursuing these topics more in-depth may wish to follow the suggestions in the 'Further Readings' sections.

The challenge from personality psychology is not only a significant challenge to virtue ethics, one which demands an answer, but it also gave us the opportunity to further examine the concept of 'character'. The challenge claims that evidence from experiments shows that there are no such things as character traits, or at least that it is situational rather than dispositional factors that affect behaviour, thus minimizing or altogether doing away with the influence of character.

While at first this seemed to be a critical point against virtue ethics, with wider devastating consequences for any theory which relies on character traits, a more careful examination of the empirical evidence showed three things. First, the interpretation of the evidence itself is under dispute even within personality psychology. Aggregation of the evidence has completely different results in terms of our ability to predict behaviour than examination of individual instances.

Second, if we accept the evidence as presented by those critical of virtue ethics, the theory can still account for the evidence by illustrating that there are many more states of character than virtue. While virtue is a stable, settled and predictable state of character, it is also a rare one. Most of us are either continent or incontinent and as a result our characters are very vulnerable to situational factors. Continence and incontinence are states of struggle and flux, we move from one state to the other depending on situational factors such as the degree of temptation or duress present in different circumstances. That is, the experiments recreate exactly the sorts of situational factors that are likely to affect dispositions, which in turn result in differing behaviours. Character traits are themselves vulnerable to situational variants. The conception of virtue as a stable, reliable disposition is a correct one, but it is also a very rare one. What should surprise us in these experiments is the number of people who got it *right* given how *rare* virtue is, rather than the number of people who got it wrong.

Finally, a more in-depth examination of the results of the experiments came up with a surprising conclusion: the experiments reveal a wealth of information about how we can 'get it wrong' and fail to act morally, all of which is very much compatible with the claims of virtue ethics as developed in this volume. So rather than being a challenge to virtue ethics, the experiments are a rich source of empirical material confirming what the virtue ethicist would expect to find in practice and a promising ground for further interdisciplinary work. The experiments also remind us that when it comes to moral matters for creatures such as ourselves, errors, failures, struggles and regress are integral parts of our development.

In Chapter 8, we continued to make reference to the evidence from personality psychology experiments in order to develop some ideas about the practical considerations involved in educating students of ethics on *how* to think rather than about *what* to think. We identified an initial difficulty in that many people fail to notice morally relevant situations in the first place, and that even this very first step of recognizing morality in practice requires sensitization. Crucial in resolving this problem is developing one's moral imagination and coming to see the world as morally active and requiring our response. We achieve this by coming to see ourselves as occupying certain roles, sharing certain values, following the example of others and, importantly, learning from the example of our teachers. The examples need not be perfect or infallible – we can learn as much from contained, small, everyday examples of morality as we can from grand gestures and we can also learn a lot from observing failure both in ourselves and others. Immersive play, the use of narrative and integrating ethics into other disciplines are all useful tools for developing moral imagination.

We then moved on to re-examine in more detail the role of emotions as they play such an important role in moral development. We identified a number of functions for the emotions:

- The world provokes emotions in us, so it's the role of education to manage the situations we come across to provoke the right emotions.

- The right emotions lead us to view the world in a particular way and alert us to the demands of morality, so it's the role of education to cultivate these emotions.

- The emotions motivate us to act and make the flow from judgement to action smooth and unproblematic, so it's the role of education to ensure that there is internal consistency and real commitment to morality.

- Finally, the emotions convey our values and judgements to others; they are a display of the genuineness of our commitment and form part of our moral judgements, so it's the role of education to deal not only with how we should think but also with how we should feel.

This chapter concluded with a look at the possibility and significance of change. One of the most interesting findings of the Milgram experiments was not so much how many people failed to act morally, but rather what lessons these subjects learnt from participating in the experiments. A closer look at Milgram's work reveals subjects who made radical and life-defining changes as a result of learning more about themselves through the experiments. Fundamentally, moral development isn't exclusively about progress, a large part of moral development is failure and how we respond to finding out that we have gone wrong. The role of education here is to manage failure, that is, to make sure that the failures we encounter are constructive and not destructive, that they lead to change and improvement, not disheartenment and defeat.

Finally, in Chapter 9, we came full circle to consider whether the account of deontological theories on which virtue ethicists based their initial objections was correct and whether modern deontologists have developed replies to these objections. Overall, the chapter demonstrated that the neo-Kantian position is far more subtle than given credit for by early virtue ethicists, but that the early criticisms have, nonetheless, served to stimulate new discussions of Kant's work and to develop Kantianism in novel ways.

The charge of rigourism, of relying on inflexible, rigid rules, has been addressed by a more detailed account of the role of the Categorical Imperative. Neo-Kantians have reinterpreted the Categorical Imperative as a test for subjective maxims, allowing room for either the formulation and/or the application of these maxims. This allows the theory to demonstrate contextual sensitivity and account for the multiplicity of morality. At the same time, neo-Kantians have refocused attention on the role of imperfect duties in Kantian theory. Imperfect duties allow room for interpretation; they allow for choice in respect to when, how and towards whom they are applied, thus responding to the virtue ethical concerns. Not only that, but they also allow room for partial considerations where appropriate, that is, where such considerations are warranted. The Kantian moral agent need not be the unpalatable moral saint, nor does she need to be committed to a life without friendships or a life lived in denial of any special concerns towards her loved ones. In this, it seems to me, that virtue ethics and neo-Kantianism have a lot in common and could probably make common cause against theories of impersonal value like some versions of consequentialism.

We then went on to reconsider the Kantian account of the emotions. Here, the picture becomes quite complicated as indeed there seem to be some passages in Kant's works that strongly suggest a deep mistrust of the emotions as pathological, corrupting influences that should be eradicated. Where there is room for the emotions, it is as specifically conceived affective responses, for example, the reverence felt for the moral law. Having said that, many neo-Kantians have attempted to rehabilitate the Kantian account of the emotions, in some cases being willing to move quite far away from other foundational Kantian ideas in doing so. We considered accounts that place some moral worth on acting from inclination alongside acting from duty, and accounts that reject inclinations as the ground of moral worth but still see some room for them when cultivated by reason. Essentially, the question of how one understands the role of emotions in Kantian thought refers back to a larger question of how one sees the relationship between the sensible and the intelligible aspects of humans.

The sensible/intelligible divide is a very complex topic in Kantian thought that gives rise to, for example, two conceptions of virtue. Sensible virtue has much in common with Aristotelian virtue, in that it is developed over time, gradually and subject to empirical contingencies. Moral worth, however, is only attributable to the intelligible virtue, the sudden revolution in perspective towards the moral law. For Aristotle, reason is central in virtue, but there is no account corresponding to the Kantian metaphysics, and the role of reason goes hand in hand with the emotions. For Kant, virtue is always struggle against untrustworthy inclinations, and although there might be some limited role for the emotions, there is no place for empirical naturalism. The conclusion of this chapter was that any comparison between the two theories on the concepts of 'virtue' and 'character' is likely to be quite a demanding project, requiring attention to detail and sensitivity to the wider theoretical considerations that shape each account.

Conclusion

Chapter 9 has been a veritable whirlwind tour of some really complex Kantian ideas, too superficial to hope to be able to capture either the intricacies of Kantian thought or the richness of neo-Kantian developments. However, within this volume, it has served an important function: it has allowed us to come full circle, from the criticisms of deontology (and consequentialism) as the status quo, to the detailed development of different accounts of virtue ethics, back to re-examining the precise nature of the disagreement between Kantians and virtue ethicists. In light of the discussions in Chapter 9, the earlier virtue ethical criticisms of deontology may seem unjustified. Some of the conceptions of deontology that thinkers like Anscombe and Williams objected to may appear to be veritable caricatures of Kant's true theory. This conclusion, however, would be unfair as it does not consider the context within which all these ideas developed. At the time when virtue ethicists called for change, the predominant conception of Kantian thought followed very much the lines thinkers like Anscombe and Williams took themselves to be objecting to. It took the virtue ethical critique to spur neo-Kantians to re-examine and redefine their own theories. When they were formulated, the criticisms were appropriate, as their target was Kantian theory as conceived at that time.

Virtue ethics as a critical movement has had more than one consequence; it has led to a revival of Aristotelian thought and increased interest in other conceptions of virtue as primary in our accounts of normativity but it has also encouraged Kantians (and to an extent consequentialists) to reconsider their own theories. Virtue ethics has shaped the landscape of modern moral philosophy in opposition to its rivals, both in virtue of its own merits and as an incentive for challenge and change in other theories. Virtue ethics as a positive movement offers us stand-alone, detailed and thought-provoking alternatives in the field of normative theories.

Although we have, in some respects, come full circle, this has not been a futile project. The process of developing these ideas has been beneficial to all thinkers involved, in that it has encouraged new questions, new approaches and new answers to familiar debates. Not only has it led to the revival of virtue ethics and the redefinition of Kantianism but it also points the way towards further debate. The central element in the account of virtue ethics as presented in this volume is the importance of moral perception and practical wisdom. The challenge for virtue ethicists now is to further develop these ideas, especially in relation to practical projects. The chapters on personality psychology, Chapter 7, and moral education, Chapter 8, tried to give an indication of the task ahead. A theory which is concerned with how one should live one's life and which places the development of practical wisdom at the heart of its deliberations should have a lot to say about the interplay between philosophy and practical disciplines such as psychology and education. Interdisciplinary work, while fashionable, is not easy to carry out successfully, but I think that the future for virtue ethics lies in clarifying the grounding of the virtues and illustrating how virtue is possible to develop in practice.

In Chapter 9, I pointed out that the greatest challenge for Aristotle is providing an account of the objective grounding of virtue, while the greatest challenge for Kant is reconciling the relationship between the empirical and the intelligible worlds. This conclusion accounts for the great interest there has been in the interplay between the two theories. Both theories have a rich account of concepts such as 'virtue' and 'character' and both theories appreciate the requirement for a strong conception of the role of reason in revealing moral requirements. At the same time the strengths of one theory are the weaknesses of the other. Where Aristotle has a very clear, plausible and persuasive account of our empirical natures, Kant struggles to reconcile two different viewpoints, sensible and intelligible, within his theory. However, where Kant has an objective account of reason as the grounding of morality, Aristotelians are still struggling to define virtue in a non-circular manner. This conclusion may seem rather depressing as the conclusion of a volume that seeks to shed light on developments in modern moral theory; however, in philosophy, the journey is often more important than the conclusion. The initial calls for change by virtue ethicists have made it possible for researchers to go on this journey of exploration and have inspired others to take up virtue ethics and to rethink Kantianism. At the end of the day, we may not have entirely clear answers on every point of either theory, but we have a much better understanding of both and of what further research is needed.

NOTES

1 Virtue ethics, a revived alternative

1 Aristotle, NE 1094b11ff.
2 Dreyfus and Dreyfus, 2005, p. 788.

2 Ethics and morality

1 Williams, 1985, p. 186.
2 Eugenides, 2011, loc 5372–81.
3 Stocker, 1997, p. 66.

3 Character and the emotions

1 Kant, G, 4:394.
2 Williams, 1985, p. 194.
3 Kant, G, 4:398.
4 Aristotle, NE 1179b19ff.
5 Burnyeat, 1980, p. 70.
6 Aristotle, NE 1103a35-b2.
7 Aristotle, NE 1103b16ff.
8 Russell, 1946, p. 185.

4 Virtue; an Aristotelian definition I

1 Driver, 2001, p. 36.
2 Driver, 2001, p. 39.

3 Watson, in Statman, 1997, p. 58.
4 Aristotle, NE 1105a27ff.
5 Aristotle, NE 1094a1.
6 Aristotle, NE 1106b35–1107a3.
7 NE 1109a26–9.
8 NE 1108b33ff.
9 All these ideas are discussed in NE Book II viii–ix.

5 Virtue; an Aristotelian definition II

1 NE 1106b35–1107a3.
2 Crombie, 1962, p. 539.
3 Annas, 1993, p. 111.
4 Wiggins in Rorty, 1980, pp. 232–3.
5 Hume, [1740] 1978, pp. 468–9.
6 Davies, 1970 (2001), p. 67.
7 Aristotle, NE 1139a 31ff.
8 Korsgaard in Engstrom and Whiting, 1996, p. 215.
9 Aristotle, NE 1144b26–7.
10 For more on all these ideas, see McDowell, 1978.
11 Hursthouse, 1999, p. 130.
12 McDowell, in Engstrom and Whiting, 1996a, p. 23.
13 McDowell, in Engstrom and Whiting, 1996a, p. 30.

6 A naturalistic account of virtue

1 Russell, 1946, p. 84.
2 Russell, 1946, p. 215.
3 Having said that, theistic versions of teleology have also seen a revival, see for example, Cottingham, in Oderberg and Chappell, 2004.
4 Sedley, 1991, p. 181.
5 For a more detailed discussion of all these arguments, see Johnson, 2005.

6   For a discussion of these kinds of objections on deriving normative precepts from nature, see, for example, Singer and Wells, 1984.

7   Annas, in Gardiner, 2005, p. 13.

8   Johnson, 2005, p. 6.

9   Aristotle, DPA, ii–iii.

10 Johnson, 2005, p. 210.

11 Aristotle, DA, I 3 406B8–10.

12 For more on all these ideas, see Johnson, 2005.

13 This example is from Annas, in Gardiner, 2005, p. 16.

14 This is Nagel's definition of moral luck, Nagel in Statman, 1993, p. 59.

15 Nagel in Statman, 1993, pp. 58–9.

16 Nussbaum, 1986, p. 5.

17 Hursthouse, 1999, p. 192.

18 Although this is too detailed an exegetical point to go into here, it is worth noting that Hursthouse's own conception of the role of the virtuous person seems to have changed over time. Her earlier works seem to indicate that virtue is defined by what the virtuous person would choose; however, her later works clearly develop and defend the kind of naturalistic account presented here.

19 Hursthouse's own term here is the 'characteristic way of going on' but I have replaced this with 'characteristic way of being' as that strikes me both as less awkward a term and as more appropriate for human beings as it refers to the agent's inner world which is expressed in action.

20 This is Annas commenting on Hursthouse's naturalism, Annas in Gardiner, 2005, p. 28.

21 Foot, 2001, pp. 16–17.

22 Geach, 1977, p. 17.

23 Foot, 1977, pp. 2–3.

7 The challenge from personality psychology

1   Sometimes also referred to as 'social psychology'.

2   Harman, 1998–99, p. 315.

3   Doris, 1998.

4   See Doris, 1998, pp. 507–8.

5 These very introductory comments can be glimpsed in any introduction to personality psychology, see, for example, Brody and Ehrlichman, 1998.

6 Brody and Ehrlichman, 1998, p. 34.

7 As an interesting aside, while the experimenters would struggle to obtain ethics approval for similar experiments nowadays, there are no such constraints on TV producers who seem to have borrowed many elements of the experiments in an attempt to make reality TV more 'entertaining'.

8 For example, Doris, 2005, p. 123.

9 See, for example, Mischel, 1968, who sees his work as challenging this existing theoretical assumption.

10 Milgram, 1974, p. 5.

11 This seems to be the gist of Mischel's attack on the dominant understanding of the importance of traits in predicting behaviour, see Mischel, 1968.

12 See Mischel 1968 and Epstein who makes this claim on behalf of Mischel in Epstein and O'Brien, 1985, p. 515.

13 This is the finding of Hartshorne and May's experiment, 1928, and also made on their behalf by Darley and Batson, 1973, p. 100.

14 Mischel, 1968, p. 283. Also, see Darley and Batson, 1973, p. 108 and Endler and Hunt, 1966, Endler and Hunt, 1968 and Endler and Hunt, 1969.

15 See, for example, an extensive discussion by Epstein, 1985.

16 Epstein, 1985, in particular, see p. 516 and p. 523.

17 Epstein, 1985, p. 533.

18 Darley and Batson, 1973, p. 108.

19 In turn see Newcomb, 1929, on extraversion, Allport and Vernon, 1933, on expressive movement and Dudycha, 1936, on punctuality. It is not clear whether these dispositions are character traits at all. Here, I am following writers such as Kupperman, 1991, who associate character with morality in some way.

20 Hartshorne and May, 1928.

21 Harman, 1998–99, p. 317.

22 NE Book 1, x.

23 Strictly speaking, this is not true; he identified six character traits, but then sets heroic virtue and bestiality aside due to their rarity, so we can also set them aside for our purposes. NE Book 7, i.

24 Furthermore, the idea that agents who are more morally mature than other, less morally mature agents, are likely to do better when faced with difficult moral tests is supported itself by psychological research itself. For example, subjects more competent at moral reasoning were found to be less likely to cheat given the opportunity on a test than those less competent (Grim et al., 1968), more likely to resist authority in order to help others (McNamee, 1977) and more likely to honour a commitment (Krebs and Rosenwald, 1977).

25 For example, Aristotle, NE 1106b 25ff.

26 Epstein, 1985, quoting Hartshorne and May, p. 523.

27 Darley and Batson, 1973, p. 108.

28 Milgram, 1974, p. 6.

29 Milgram, 1974, p. 10.

30 Milgram, 1974, p. 10.

8 Moral education and the virtues

1 Doris, 1998, pp. 511–13.

2 Doris and Stitch, 2005, p. 120.

3 There is an element of luck here, as we saw in Chapter 6 Section C, extreme bad luck may lead to the development of vicious character traits, but for those of us fortunate enough to escape *extremely* adverse influences, education will make all the difference.

4 Darley and Bateson, pp. 107–8.

5 Admittedly, this is purely anecdotal evidence so its value may be limited, but this was not an isolated example in my experience of teaching in a medical school. Furthermore, other authors cite similar examples, for example, Sokol, 2012, p. 3.

6 Hinnman in Brown 2000, p. 413.

7 Warnock, 1978, p. 196.

8 Sherman, in Carr and Steutel, 1999, p. 37.

9 Sherman, in Carr and Steutel, 1999, p. 41.

10 For more on the importance of teachers and their conduct in character education, see Buber 1965, Bennett 1991 and Wynn 1991.

11 Lickona in Callahan and Bok, 1980, p. 131.

12 Milgram, 1974, p. 36.

13 Lickona in Callahan and Bok, 1980, p. 130.

14 Aristotle, R, 1378a8.
15 Sherman, in Carr and Steutel, 1999, p. 40.
16 All these ideas are developed by Aristotle in the *Rhetoric*, Part II.
17 Milgram, 1974, p. 52.
18 Milgram, 1974, p. 54.
19 Milgram, 1974, p. 196.

9 The Kantian response

1 Wood, 2006, p. 8.
2 Kant, G 4:421.
3 O'Neill, 1989, p. 97.
4 Another author who has a similar approach, arguing that the concept of the Categorical Imperative has built in qualifications, is Hill, in Beltzer, 2008, pp. 39–40.
5 Wood, 2008, p. 152.
6 Wood, 2008, p. 60.
7 Wood, 2008, p. 63.
8 For this argument, see Baron, in Bird, 2006, pp. 340–1. The reference to the KpV is 5:158.
9 Baron, in Beltzer, 2008, p. 253.
10 NE, Book 5.
11 Baron, in Beltzer, 2008, p. 253.
12 I am extremely grateful to David McNaughton and Piers Rawlings for inspiring these thoughts on impartiality/partiality in an, as yet unpublished, paper entitled 'Impartiality and duties of special relationships', given at the Ratio conference at Reading University.
13 Kant, KpV 5:74.
14 Kant, MS 6:399, and for the following discussion, see also 6:400–3.
15 For such an account of Kantian feelings, see, for example, Anderson, in Beltzer, 2008.
16 Wood, 2008, pp. 35–6.
17 Baron et al., 1997, p. 58.
18 Baxley, 2003, pp. 557–8. A similar account of feelings prompting us to action can be found in Baron, 1995.
19 Kant, KpV, 5:72–3.

20 Kant, MS, 6:394 and 397.

21 Kant, KpV, 5:38.

22 Kant, KpV, 5:76–7.

23 Kant, MS, 6:383–4.

24 Kant, A 254.

25 Kant, MS, 6:480.

26 See the seminal Korsgaard, in Engstrom and Whiting, 1996.

BIBLIOGRAPHY

Allport, G. W. and Vernon, P. E., 1933, *Studies in Expressive Movement*, New York: Macmillan.

Anderson, E., 2008, 'Emotions in Kant's Later Moral Philosophy', in Beltzer M. (ed.), *Kant's Ethic of Virtue*, Berlin: Walter de Gruyter.

Andre, J., 1993, 'Nagel, Williams and Moral Luck', in Statman D. (ed.), *Moral Luck*, Albany, NY: State University of New York Press.

Annas, J., 1993, *The Morality of Happiness*, Oxford: Oxford University Press.

— 2003, 'Virtue Ethics and Social Psychology', *A Priori: The Erskine Lectures in Philosophy*, https://kb.osu.edu/dspace/handle/1811/32006.

— 2005, 'Virtue Ethics: What Kind of Naturalism?', in Gardiner S. (ed.), *Virtue Ethics Old and New*, New York: Cornell University Press.

— 2011, *Intelligent Virtue*, Oxford: Oxford University Press.

Anscombe, G. E. M., 1958, 'Modern Moral Philosophy', *Philosophy*, 33(124): 1–16, reprinted in Crisp R. and Slote M., 1997, *Virtue Ethics*, Oxford: Oxford University Press.

Arthur, J., 2008, 'Traditional Approaches to Character Education in Britain and America', in Nucci L. P. and Narvaez D. (eds), *The Handbook of Moral and Character Education*, Kindle edition.

Athanassoulis, N., 2000, 'A Response to Harman', *Proceedings of the Aristotelian Society*, 100: 215–21.

— 2005, *Morality, Moral Responsibility and Moral Luck*, Basingstoke: Palgrave.

— 2007, 'Training Good Professionals: Ethics and Health Care Education', in Ashcroft, Dawson, Draper and McMillan (eds), Gillon's *Principles of Health Care Ethics*, Chichester: Willey and Sons.

Baron, M. W., 1995, *Kantian Ethics Almost Without Apology*, New York: Cornell University Press.

— 2006, 'Moral Paragons and the Metaphysics of Morals', in Bird G. (ed.), *A Companion to Kant*, Oxford: Blackwell.

— 2008, 'Virtue Ethics, Kantian Ethics and the "One Thought Too Many" Objection', in Beltzer M. (ed.), *Kant's Ethic of Virtue*, Berlin: Walter de Gruyter.

Baron, M. W., Pettit, P. and Slote, M., 1997, *Three Methods of Ethics*, Oxford: Blackwell.

Baxley, A. M., 2003, 'Does Kantian Virtue Amount to More than Continence?', *The Review of Metaphysics*, 56: 559–86.

Beltzer, M., 2008, *Kant's Ethic of Virtue*, Berlin: Walter de Gruyter.

Bennett, W. J., 1991, 'Moral Literacy and the Formation of Character', in Bennings J. (ed.), *Moral Character and Civic Education in the Elementary School*, New York: Teachers College Press.

Brody, N. and Ehrlichman, H., 1998, *Personality Psychology*, New Jersey: Prentice Hall.

Buber, M., 1965, *Between Man and Man*, New York: Macmillan.

Buckle, S., 1991, 'Natural Law', in Singer P. (ed.), *A Companion to Ethics*, Oxford: Blackwell.

Burnyeat, M. F., 1980, 'Aristotle on Learning to be Good', in Rorty A. O. (ed.), *Essays on Aristotle's Ethics*, Berkeley, CA: University of California Press.

Carr, D., 2008, 'Character Education as the Cultivation of Virtue', in Nucci L. P. and Narvaez D. (eds), *The Handbook of Moral and Character Education*, Kindle edition.

Carr, D. and Steutel, J., 1999, *Virtue Ethics and Moral Education*, Abington: Routledge.

Chappell, T., 'Bernard Williams', *The Stanford Encyclopaedia of Philosophy*, (Fall 2010 Edition), Edward N. Zalta (ed.), URL=http://plato.stanford.edu/archives/fall2010/entries/williams-bernard/.

Cottingham, J., 1996, 'Partiality and the Virtues', in Crisp R. (ed.), *How Should One Live?*, Oxford: Clarendon Press.

—2004, '"Our Natural Guide . . .": Conscience, "Nature", and Moral Experience', in D. Oderberg and T. Chappell (eds), *Human Values*, London: Palgrave.

Crombie, I. M., 1962, 'An Exegetical Point in Aristotle's *Nicomachean Ethics*', *Mind*, 284: 539–40.

Dancy, J., 2004, *Ethics Without Principles*, Oxford: Oxford University Press.

Darley, J. M. and Batson, C. D., 1973, '"From Jerusalem to Jericho": A Study of Situational and Dispositional Variables in Helping Behavior', *Journal of Personality and Social Psychology*, 27(1): 100–8.

Davies, R. W., [1970] 2001, *The Depthford Trilogy: Fifth Business*, Toronto: Penguin.

DePaul, M., 1999, 'Character Traits, Virtues and Vices: Are There None?', *Proceedings of the 20th World Congress of Philosophy*, Bowling Green, Ohio: Philosophy Documentation Center.

Doris, J. M., 1998, 'Persons, Situations and Virtue Ethics', *Nous*, 32(4): 504–40.

—2002, *Lack of Character: Personality and Moral Behaviour*, Cambridge: Cambridge University Press.

Doris, J. and Stich, S. P., 2005, 'As a Matter of Fact: Empirical Perspectives on Ethics', in Smith M. and Jackson F. (eds), *The Oxford Handbook in Contemporary Philosophy*, Oxford: Oxford University Press.

Dreyfus, H. and Dreyfus, S., 2005, 'Expertise in Real World Contexts', *Organization Studies*, 26(5): 779–92.

Driver, J., 2001, *Uneasy Virtue*, Cambridge: Cambridge University Press.

Dudycha, G. J., 1936, 'An Objective Study of Punctuality', *Archives of Psychology*, 29: 1–53.

Endler, N. S. and Hunt, J. M., 1966, 'Sources of Behavioural Variance as Measured by the S-R Inventory of Anxiousness', *Psychological Bulletin*, 65: 336–46.

—1968, 'S-R Inventories of Hostility and Comparisons of the Proportions of Variance from Persons, Responses and Situations for Hostility and Anxiousness', *Journal of Personality and Social Psychology*, 9(4): 309–15.

— 1969, "Generalizability of contributions from sources of variance in the S-R inventories of anxiousness", *Journal of Personality*, 37(1): 1–24.

Epstein, S. and O'Brien, E. J., 1985, 'The Person-Situation Debate in Historical and Current Perspective', *Psychological Bulletin*, 98(3): 513–37.

Eugenides, J., 2011, *The Marriage Plot*, Kindle edition.

Foot, P., 1972, 'Morality as a System of Hypothetical Imperatives', *Philosophical Review*, 81(3): 305–16.

—1977, *Virtues and Vices*, Oxford: Clarendon Press.

—2001, *Natural Goodness*, Oxford: Clarendon Press.

Geach, P., 1977, *The Virtues*, Cambridge: Cambridge University Press.

Grim, P., Kohlberg, L. and White, S., 1968, 'Some Relationships between Conscience and Attentional Processes', *Journal of Personality and Social Psychology*, 8: 239–52.

Harman, G., 1998–9, 'Moral Philosophy Meets Social Psychology: Virtue Ethics and the Fundamental Attribution Error', *Proceedings of the Aristotelian Society*, 99: 315–31.

Hartman, E. M., 2000, 'An Aristotelian Approach to Moral Imagination', *Professional Ethics,* 8: 57–77.

Hartshorne, H. and May, M. A., 1928, *Studies in the Nature of Character*, Vol. 1, *Studies in deceit*, New York: Macmillan.

Hill, E. H., 2008, in Beltzer, M. (ed.), *Kant's Ethic of Virtue*, Berlin: Walter de Gruyter.

Hinnman, L., 2000, 'Seeing Wisely: Learning to Become Wise', in Brown W. S. (ed.), *Understanding Wisdom*, Pennsylvania, PA: Templeton Foundation Press.

Hull, D. L., 1998, 'On Human Nature', in Hull D. L. and Ruse M. (eds),
  The Philosophy of Biology, Oxford: Clarendon Press.
Hume, D., [1740], 1978, *A Treatise of Human Nature III*, Oxford:
  Oxford University Press.
Hunt, J. M., 1969, 'Generalizability of Contributions from Sources of
  Variance in the S-R Inventories of Anxiousness', *Journal of Personality*,
  37(1): 1–24.
Hursthouse, R., 1997, 'Virtue Theory and Abortion', in Crisp R. and Slote
  M. (eds), *Virtue Ethics*, Oxford: Oxford University Press.
— 1999, *On Virtue Ethics*, Oxford: Oxford University Press.
— 2006, 'The Central Doctrine of the Mean', in Kraut R. (ed.), *The
  Blackwell Guide to Aristotle's Nicomachean Ethics*, Oxford: Blackwell.
Johnson, M. R., 2005, *Aristotle on Teleology*, Oxford: Clarendon Press.
Kagan, S., 1989, *The Limits of Morality*, Oxford: Oxford University Press.
Kamtekar, R., 2004, 'Situationism and Virtue Ethics on the Content of our
  Character', *Ethics*, 114: 458–91.
Kekes, J., 1991, 'Moral Imagination, Freedom and the Humanities',
  American Philosophical Quarterly, 28(22): 101–11.
Kitcher, P., 1999, 'Essence and Perfection', *Ethics*, 100: 59–83.
Korsgaard, C. M., 1996, 'From Duty and for the Sake of the Noble',
  in Engstrom S. and Whiting J. (eds), *Aristotle, Kant and the Stoics:
  Rethinking Happiness and Duty*, Cambridge: Cambridge University Press.
Krebs, D. and Rosenwald, A., 1977, 'Moral Reasoning and Moral Behaviour
  in Conventional Adults', *Merrill Palmer Wuarterly*, 23: 77–87.
Kupperman, J. J., 1991, *Character*, Oxford: Oxford University Press.
— 2001, 'The Indispensability of Character', *Philosophy*, 76: 239–50.
Lawrence, G., 2006, 'Human Good and Human Function', in Kraut R.
  (ed.), *The Blackwell Guide to Aristotle's Nicomachean Ethics*, Oxford:
  Blackwell.
Lenman, J., 'Ethical Naturalism', *The Stanford Encyclopedia of
  Philosophy (Winter 2009 Edition)*, Edward N. Zalta (ed.), http://plato.
  stanford.edu/archives/win2009/entries/naturalism-moral/.
Lickona, T., 1980, 'What Does Moral Psychology Have to Say to the
  Teacher of Ethics?', in Callahan D., and Bok S. (eds), *Ethics Teaching
  in Higher Education*, New York: Plenum Press.
Louden, R., 1997, 'Some Vices of Virtue Ethics', in Statman D. (ed.), *Virtue
  Ethics: A Critical Reader*, Edinburgh: Edinburgh University Press.
MacIntyre, A. C., 1981, *After Virtue*, Notre Dame, IN: Notre Dame Press.
McDowell, J., 1996a, 'Deliberation and Moral Development', in Engstrom
  S. and Whiting J. (eds), *Aristotle, Kant and the Stoics: Rethinking
  Happiness and Duty*, Cambridge: Cambridge University Press.
— 1996b, 'Incontinence and Practical Wisdom in Aristotle', in Lovibond S.
  and Williams S. G. (eds), *Essays for David Wiggins: Identity, Truth and
  Value*, Aristotelian Society Series Vol. 16.

— 1978, 'Are Moral Requirements Hypothetical Imperatives?', *Proceedings of the Aristotelian Society*, 52: 13–29.

— 1979, 'Virtue and Reason', *The Monist*, 62: 331–50.

— 1980, 'The Role of Eudaimonia in Aristotle's Ethics', in Rorty A. O. (ed.), *Essays on Aristotle's Ethics*, Berkeley, CA: University of California Press.

McNamee, S., 1977, 'Moral Behaviour, Moral Development and Motivation', *Journal of Moral Education*, 7: 27–31.

Merritt, M., 2000, 'Virtue Ethics and Situationist Personality Psychology', *Ethical Theory and Moral Practice*, 3: 365–83.

Milgram, S., 1974, *Obedience to Authority*, New York: Harper & Row.

Mischel, W., 1968, *Personality and Assessment*, USA: John Wiley and Sons.

Montmarquet, J., 2003, 'Moral Character and Social Science Research', *Philosophy*, 78(3): 355–68.

Nagel, T., 1976, 'Moral Luck', *Proceedings of the Aristotelian Society*, 50: 137–51.

Newcomb, T. M., 1929, *Consistency of Certain Extrovert-Introvert Behavior Patterns in 51 Problem Boys*, New York: Columbia University.

Nussbaum, M., 1986, *The Fragility of Goodness*, Cambridge: Cambridge University Press.

O'Neill, O., 1989, *Constructions of Reason*, Cambridge: Cambridge University Press.

Pardales, M., 2002, 'So How Did You Arrive at that Decision? Connecting Moral Imagination and Moral Judgment', *Journal of Moral Education*, 31(4): 423–37.

Roberts, R. C., 1991, 'Virtues and Rules', *Philosophy and Phenomenological Research*, 51(2): 325–43.

Ross, W. D., 1931, *The Right and the Good*, Oxford: Clarendon Press.

Russell, B., 1946 (1991), *History of Western Philosophy*, England: Routledge.

Russell, D. C., 2009, *Practical Intelligence and the Virtues*, Oxford: Clarendon Press.

Sedley, D., 1991, 'Is Aristotle's Teleology Anthropocentric?', *Phronesis*, 36(2): 179–96.

Sherman, N., 1989, *The Fabric of Character*, Oxford: Clarendon Press.

— 1997, *Making a Necessity of Virtue*, Cambridge: Cambridge University Press.

— 1999, 'Character Development', in Carr D. and Steutel J. (eds), *Virtue Ethics and Moral Education*, London: Routledge.

Singer, P. and Wells, D., 1984, *The Reproduction Revolution*, Oxford: Oxford University Press.

Sokol, D., 2012, *Doing Clinical Ethics*, Dordrecht: Springer.

Solomon, D., 1997, 'Internal Objections to Virtue Ethics', in Statman D. (ed.), *Virtue Ethics: A Critical Reader*, Edinburgh: Edinburgh University Press.

Sreenivasan, G., 2002, 'Errors About Errors: Virtue Theory and Trait Attribution', *Mind*, 111(441): 47–68.

Statman, D., 1993, *Moral Luck*, Albany, NY: State University of New York Press.

Stocker, M., 1976, 'The Schizophrenia of Modern Ethical Theories', *Journal of Philosophy*, 73: 453–66, reprinted in Crisp R. and Slote M., 1997, *Virtue Ethics*, Oxford: Oxford University Press.

Stohr, K. and Wellman, C. H., 2002, 'Recent Work on Virtue Ethics', *American Philosophical Quarterly*, 39(1): 49–72.

Sturgeon, N. L., 2006, 'Ethical Naturalism', in Copp D. (ed.), *The Oxford Handbook of Ethical Theory*, Oxford: Oxford University Press.

Urmson, J. O., 1980, 'Aristotle's Doctrine of the Mean', in Rorty A. O. (ed.), *Essays on Aristotle's Ethics*, Berkeley, CA: University of California Press.

Warnock, M., 1978, *Imagination*, Berkeley, CA: University of California Press.

Watson, G., 1997, 'On the Primacy of Character', in Statman D. (ed.), *Virtue Ethics: A Critical Reader*, Edinburgh: Edinburgh University Press.

Wiggins, D., 1980, 'Deliberation and Practical Reason', in Rorty A. O. (ed.), *Essays on Aristotle's Ethics*, Berkeley, CA: University of California Press.

Williams, B., 1973, 'Ethical Consistency', in his *Problems of the Self*, Cambridge: Cambridge University Press.

—1976, 'Moral Luck', *Proceedings of the Aristotelian Society*, 50: 115–35.

—1981a, 'Moral Luck', in his *Moral Luck*, Cambridge: Cambridge University Press.

—1981b, 'Persons, Character and Morality', in his *Moral Luck*, Cambridge: Cambridge University Press.

—1985, *Ethics and the Limits of Philosophy*, London: Fontana Press.

Wolf, S., 1982, 'Moral Saints', *Journal of Philosophy*, 79: 419–39, reprinted in Crisp R. and Slote M., 1997, *Virtue Ethics*, Oxford: Oxford University Press.

Wood, A. W., 1999, *Kant's Ethical Thought,* Cambridge: Cambridge University Press.

—2006, 'The Supreme Principle of Morality', http://www.stanford.edu/~allenw/webpapers/SupremePrincipleMorality.pdf, accessed 16 January 2012.

—2008, *Kantian Ethics*, Cambridge: Cambridge University Press.

Wynne, E. A., 1991, 'Character and Academics in the Elementary School' in Bennings J. (ed.), *Moral Character and Civic Education in the Elementary School*, New York: Teachers College Press.

INDEX

agent regret   34
Anscombe, Elizabeth   11–14, 23, 48, 157
Aristotle   4, 6–7, 14–16, 29, 41–6, 54, 57–61, 65, 70–1, 73, 76–8, 80–93, 98, 103, 107–8, 113–14, 117, 119, 121, 127, 129, 131–2, 138, 142–3, 145, 148–51, 156–8

Baron, Marcia   141–3, 146
Batson, C. D.   118–19
Baxley, Margaret   146
beneficence   25–6, 37–8, 88, 146
benevolence *see* beneficence
Braveman, Morris   134
Byrnyeat, M. F.   42

Categorical Imperative   8, 12, 16, 24, 70, 137–43, 155
compassion *see* kindness
consequences *see* consequentialism
consequentialism   4, 11–14, 16, 29, 31–3, 35–6, 44, 48, 50, 53–4, 58, 67, 69–70, 88, 98, 155, 157
continence *see* weakness of will
courage   37, 61, 63–4, 78–9, 95

Darley, J. M.   118–19
deontology   4, 8, 11–14, 16, 31–3, 35, 44, 48, 50, 53–5, 58, 67, 69–70, 98

dishonesty *see* honesty
disposition(s)   26, 36, 44, 55, 58, 61, 76–9, 96, 107–10, 112, 116, 122, 127, 153
Doctrine of the Mean   6, 61–6, 68–9, 99, 119, 126
Doris, John   104, 107–8, 110–11, 121–2
Driver, Julia   55
duty   11–12, 14, 138–9, 141–7, 155

Eichmann, Adolf   134
Epstein, Robert   110
eudaimonia   5, 14, 59–61, 94–5

flourishing see *eudaimonia*
Foot, Philippa   6, 81, 85, 93, 95–6, 99
friendship   5, 12, 20, 23–5, 30, 32–3, 40, 42, 45–6, 50, 71–5, 88, 93, 113, 127, 133, 142–3, 149, 151, 155
function argument   6, 35, 58–61, 66, 80–8, 94, 98–9

Geach, Peter   95
Good Samaritan experiment   105–7, 110–11, 116, 118–19, 122–3, 129

good will   35, 147–8
gratitude   25–7
Greatest Happiness
      principle   12, 16

habit   41–2, 68, 78–80, 109, 118,
      133, 135, 147–9
Harman, Gilbert   104, 107,
      110–12, 114
Hartshorne, H.   111, 116–18
Herman, Barbara   140
Hinnman, Lawrence   125
honesty   17–18, 20, 107, 111,
      117–18
honour   59–60, 130
Hume   4, 54, 73–4, 77
Hursthouse, Rosalind   6, 81, 85,
      93–5, 99

impartiality *see* partiality
incontinence *see* weakness
      of will
injustice *see* justice

justice   25, 29, 34, 43–6, 57, 79,
      96, 142

Kant   6, 8, 12, 14, 23–4,
      35–9, 41, 44–5, 50, 91,
      99, 103, 137–51, 155–9
Kantian theory *see* deontology;
      Kant
kindness   40, 42, 44–5, 57–8, 73,
      79, 91, 107, 112–13, 126,
      129–32, 144

law conception of ethics   12–13,
      34, 48
luck   27, 36, 46, 49, 122
   moral   85, 88–93, 97
lying   17–18, 139–41

May, M. A.   111, 116–18
Milgram, Stanley   109, 133, 154
Milgram experiments   105–6,
      116, 119, 129, 134, 154
moral law   8, 145, 151, 155
moral saint(s)   30–1, 141–2, 155

Nagel, Thomas   89–90
narrative   128, 136, 154
Nietzsche   4, 54, 69

O'Neill, Onora   139
obligation(s)   4–5, 12, 14, 23–7,
      33–4, 48–9, 118, 129
'one thought too many'
      argument   33–4

partiality   28–30, 34, 88,
      142–3, 155
personality   39
Plato   4, 54
pleasure   59
Priam   92
prima facie duties   23–5,
      34, 140
pro tanto reasons   34
promise keeping   23–5

relativism   16
righteous indignation   63, 131, 133
role play   128, 154
Ross, W. D.   23–5
rules
   moral   4–5, 8, 12, 17–21,
      46, 64, 67–8, 70–1, 75,
      138–46, 155
Russell, Bertrand   46, 82–3

Sedley, David   83
Sherman, Nancy   127, 131
sympathy *see* kindness

truthfulness *see* honesty; lying

Utilitarianism   12, 16, 31–2,
    35, 142
utility *see* Utilitarianism

vice   7
virtuous agent   6
voluntariness   37, 39, 89

Warnock, Mary   126
Watson, Gary   55, 59
weakness of will   7, 114–17,
    119–21, 150, 153
wealth   60
Wiggins, David   73
Williams, Bernard   22–7, 33,
    35–6, 48–9, 89, 157
Wood, Allen   140, 145